THE SILENT WITNESS: THE UNSOLVED MURDER OF MARY ROGERS

A Scandal That Shook New York and Inspired Edgar Allan Poe

SHADOWS OF THE PAST
BOOK II

ELIZA HAWTHORNE

COPYRIGHT

TABLE OF CONTENTS

INTRODUCTION

The year was 1841, and Mary Rogers, known far and wide as the "Beautiful Cigar Girl," was the talk of New York City. With her striking features and enigmatic smile, she not only charmed the patrons of her mother's tobacco shop but also the city's burgeoning media. Mary's role as a cigar saleswoman placed her at odds with the "Cult of True Womanhood," a set of ideals that insisted women be passive, pure, and confined to the home. Her life embodied the tension between societal expectations and personal independence, making her both a curiosity and a subject of fascination.

It was more than her charm that set tongues wagging. In July of that year, Mary vanished. Her absence was a sudden void, and the city buzzed with rumors and speculation. When her lifeless body was found floating in the Hudson River, the public's fascination turned to horror. The mystery of her death, filled with unanswered questions, captured the imagination of a city already gripped by the rapid changes of urban life. New York City in the 1840s was a place of extremes; rapid urbanization brought throngs of people and an explosion of businesses. At the same time, crime and vice simmered beneath the surface, just out of the reach of an overburdened police force.

Mary Rogers' murder was a watershed moment for the newspapers, who saw in her story the perfect scandal to feed an eager public. Here was a beautiful young woman who defied societal norms and met a tragic, mysterious end. The press, capitalizing on the public's fascination, spun tales and theories that often overshadowed the facts. Sensational journalism was on the rise, and Mary's case played a pivotal role in shaping the emerging media landscape, where scandal and intrigue were used to sell papers, blurring the line between news and fiction. This case marked a turning point in how the media exploited crime stories to captivate audiences, reflecting societal anxieties and moral debates of the time.

Yet, the significance of Mary Rogers' case extends beyond the lurid headlines. It represents a turning point in American history, where the intersection of media, gender roles, and forensic science became painfully apparent. Her murder revealed the limitations of forensic methods in the early 19th century; a time when the tools to investigate such crimes were still in their infancy, often speculative rather than scientific. The case highlighted the gap between public expectations and the law's capabilities, forcing the nascent criminal justice system to confront its inadequacies.

In *The Silent Witness: The Unsolved Murder of Mary Rogers*, we embark on a comprehensive exploration of the life and death of Mary Rogers. We will dissect the sensational journalism that both fueled and hindered the investigation, the gender dynamics that played a critical role in how Mary was perceived and treated, and the early forensic practices that struggled to make sense of her death. This book is not just a retelling of a historical event but a meticulous investigation into the broader societal implications of Mary Rogers' case.

As part of the *Shadows of the Past* series, this book follows a unique narrative approach that combines scholarly research with engaging storytelling. Whether you're a true crime fan or a history enthusiast, *The Silent Witness* will draw you into the bustling streets of 19th-century New York. In this city, societal pressures, gender dynamics, and burgeoning forensic practices collided in the most tragic of ways.

Allow me to introduce myself. I am Eliza Hawthorne, a historian and true crime author with a deep passion for uncovering the mysteries of the past. I specialize in 19th and early 20th-century crimes, and my work has been recognized for its rigorous historical research and immersive narrative style. When I'm not poring over archives or writing, you'll often find me exploring historical sites, searching for hidden truths.

In the chapters that follow, we will step into the labyrinth of Mary Rogers' life and death. We will start with her early years and her rise to public attention as the "Beautiful Cigar Girl." From there, we will delve into the night of her disappearance and the subsequent discovery of her body. Each chapter will explore different facets of the investigation, the media frenzy, and the societal impact of her murder. We will also consider the key suspects and prevailing theories that have emerged over the years.

This journey will not only reveal the complexities of the case but also shed light on them. Still, it will also reflect broader themes in American history, from the evolution of forensic science to the role of women in society. As we uncover the story of Mary Rogers, a woman whose life and death continue to resonate, you'll gain a deeper understanding of the limitations of justice in the 19th century and the enduring impact of her case.

So, dear reader, I invite you to walk alongside me through the bustling streets of 1840s New York. Let us uncover the story of Mary Rogers, a woman who defied the expectations of her time and whose mysterious death continues to captivate the world. The mystery awaits.

CHAPTER 1

THE LIFE OF MARY ROGERS

In a bustling New York City tobacco shop, Mary Rogers stood out not just for her beauty but for her poise and charm. To the regulars, she was a familiar face, the 'Beautiful Cigar Girl' whose presence added an air of elegance to the otherwise smoky, masculine environment. But behind her captivating smile lay a story of remarkable resilience and ambition, shaped by the formidable challenges of her early life. Mary's journey was a testament to the human spirit, a young woman navigating a world that often seemed set against her, yet never losing her grace or determination. Her resilience in the face of adversity is a source of inspiration for us all.

Early Life and Family Background

Mary Cecilia Rogers was born in 1820 in New York, a city on the cusp of enormous change. Both love and loss marked her early years. When Mary was just five years old, her father passed away, leaving her mother to support the family. Mary's mother, Phoebe Rogers, was a resourceful woman who managed a boarding house, a common means of livelihood for many widows of the time. The boarding house was more than a place of business; it was a home filled with the comings and goings of various tenants, each bringing their own stories and struggles. This environment fostered in Mary a sense of resilience and adaptability early on in life.

Growing up without a father figure, Mary developed a close bond with her mother. Phoebe was both a guiding force and a pillar of strength for Mary, instilling in her daughter the values of hard work and perseverance. Together, they faced the economic challenges of running a boarding house, the uncertainty of income, and the ever-present need to make ends meet. These experiences shaped Mary's character, teaching her the importance of self-reliance and determination. Despite the financial struggles, Phoebe ensured that Mary received a basic education, which was more than many girls of her socioeconomic status could hope for at the time.

Despite the challenges they faced, the bond between Mary and her mother was unshakeable. Phoebe was more than just a caretaker; she was Mary's emotional anchor in a world full of uncertainties. Together, they shared quiet moments of solace in the boarding house, where Phoebe would tell stories of resilience and remind Mary of the strength they both carried. These moments of intimacy were rare but precious, providing Mary with the emotional foundation she would rely on as she entered the public sphere. Phoebe's unwavering support taught Mary that, even when the world seemed harsh, family and love could offer a lifeline.

In the early 19th century, societal norms dictated that women should be pious, pure, submissive, and domestic. These ideals, often referred to as the 'Cult of True Womanhood,' placed immense pressure on young women like Mary to conform to rigid expectations. Women were expected to focus on home and family, with limited opportunities for education or employment outside the domestic sphere. However, Mary's involvement in the tobacco shop would later position her as an anomaly in this cultural landscape. Her role challenged the conventional image of womanhood, making her both a subject of admiration and scrutiny. She defied the norms of her time, becoming a working woman in a male-dominated space, and her struggles became a source of empathy for the audience. Her role in the tobacco shop is a testament to her courage and the power of individual choice in the face of societal norms.

For Mary, navigating the confines of the 'Cult of True Womanhood' was a constant battle. While society expected women to remain within the domestic sphere, focusing solely on family and virtue, Mary's ambitions stretched far beyond these narrow expectations. Her role in the tobacco shop positioned her as an anomaly; a woman who was both admired for her beauty and criticized for stepping outside traditional roles. The tension between her desire for independence and the rigid societal ideals surrounding women created internal conflicts. On one hand, she longed for respect and autonomy; on the other, she felt the weight of public judgment pressing against her every move.

Mary's childhood was not without its share of significant events that left an indelible mark on her. The death of her father was a profound loss that forced her to grow up quickly. But there were also moments of joy and warmth in the boarding house, where the sense of community provided a semblance of stability. One such memory that Mary often cherished was the annual summer fair held in their neighborhood. It was a day when the usually somber streets came alive with colors, music, and laughter. Mary, with her mother by her side, would stroll through the fair, savoring the rare moments of carefree joy. These experiences, though few and far between, nurtured a sense of hope and ambition in young Mary.

As Mary grew older, her personality began to reflect the lessons learned from her formative years. She was known for her kindness and social skills, traits that endeared her to the boarding house tenants and later to the customers of the tobacco shop. Her resilience shone through in her ability to handle the demanding responsibilities of helping her mother, all while maintaining a positive outlook. Mary's ambition, evident in her desire to rise above her circumstances and seek opportunities to assert her independence in a society that offered limited avenues for women, is a testament to her determination and a source of inspiration for the audience. Her ambition is a reminder that we can all strive for more, even in the face of adversity.

The challenges of Mary's upbringing, coupled with the societal norms of the time, played a crucial role in shaping her future choices. Her early life was a testament to the strength and resilience that defined her character. As we delve deeper into her story, we will see how these qualities, forged in the crucible of hardship and societal expectations, influenced every aspect of her life. They influenced her decision to work at the tobacco shop, her interactions with the public, and her resilience in the face of intense scrutiny. These factors led her to become the enigmatic figure who captured the imagination of 19th-century New York.

Mary Rogers as the "Beautiful Cigar Girl"

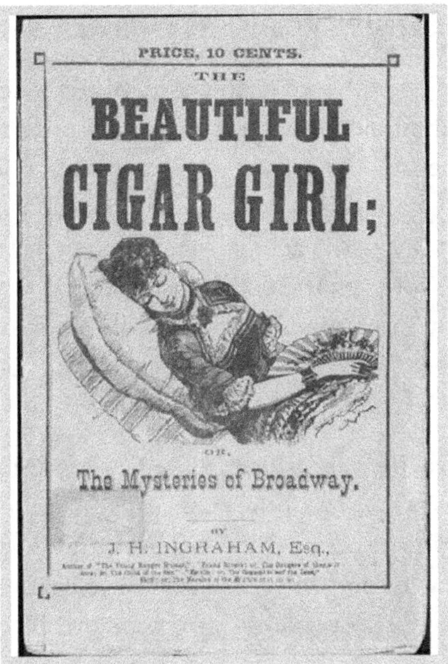

Mary Rogers' transformation into the "Beautiful Cigar Girl" was not just a change in employment; it was a shift that catapulted her into the public eye, making her both a beloved figure and a subject of intense scrutiny. Employed at John Anderson's tobacco shop, Mary's role was far from ordinary. Her job involved more than just selling cigars; it required her to engage with a diverse clientele, including businessmen, sailors, and even the occasional celebrity. The shop, strategically located in the bustling heart of New York City, became a magnet for those drawn not only by the quality of the cigars but also by the charm of the young woman behind the counter.

Though Mary was admired for her beauty and grace, she faced numerous challenges in her public role. One story often shared by those who knew her involved a regular customer who frequently made inappropriate advances. While many women would have recoiled in fear, Mary managed the situation with remarkable poise. She politely yet firmly maintained her boundaries, using her charm to defuse the tension without compromising her dignity. This anecdote reveals her ability to navigate uncomfortable and sometimes dangerous situations while remaining composed; a skill she honed over the years as she learned to manage the public's conflicting expectations of her as both a woman and a worker.

Mary's daily tasks at the tobacco shop were a blend of routine and interaction. She meticulously arranged the cigars, maintaining an air of sophistication in the shop. However, it was her interactions with customers that truly defined her role. Her ability to engage in intelligent and warm conversations with each patron, whether they were businessmen, sailors, or even the occasional celebrity, set her apart. These interactions not only showcased her social skills but also her resilience in a male-dominated space. The societal expectations of the time clashed with her public role, making her both an icon and a target.

The media's portrayal of Mary Rogers played a significant role in shaping her public image. Newspapers of the time, eager to capitalize on her beauty and the novelty of her position, often featured her in their pages. Illustrations of Mary, accompanied by florid descriptions, painted her as an ethereal figure, almost otherworldly in her allure. The fascination with her looks overshadowed her personal struggles and aspirations. This objectification not only heightened her public visibility but also added layers of vulnerability to her already precarious position.

The fascination with Mary's appearance often came at a cost. Gender dynamics of the era meant that a woman in a public-facing job was subjected to constant scrutiny and judgment. The expectations placed on women to be paragons of virtue and modesty were in direct conflict with the reality of Mary's work. Instances of harassment were not uncommon, as some patrons saw her role as an invitation for unwanted advances. The public's gaze was both adoring and predatory, a duality that Mary had to navigate with grace and resilience.

Mary's job at the tobacco shop inevitably influenced her personal life. Her interactions with regular customers and coworkers formed the fabric of her social network. Among her coworkers, she was often seen as a confidante and friend, someone who could be relied upon for a kind word or a shared laugh. Yet, the very visibility that made her a beloved figure also complicated her romantic prospects. Her relationship with Daniel

Payne, her fiancé, was marked by both affection and tension, the latter often fueled by the pressures and gossip surrounding her role.

The tobacco shop was a microcosm of the larger societal dynamics at play. Mary's charm and professionalism won her many admirers, but it also placed her under a microscope. Every smile, every friendly gesture was dissected by a public eager for scandal. This relentless scrutiny seeped into her personal relationships, creating strains that were hard to mend. Friends and acquaintances, well-meaning or otherwise, often projected their own expectations onto Mary, making it difficult for her to find solace even in her private moments.

Mary Rogers' life as the "Beautiful Cigar Girl" was a delicate balancing act. She navigated the line between public admiration and personal vulnerability with remarkable poise. Her role at the tobacco shop, while offering her a semblance of independence, also exposed her to the harsh realities of gendered expectations and societal scrutiny. The media's portrayal of her, both adoring and objectifying, added layers of complexity to her existence. In the end, it was this very visibility that contributed to the tragic end of a young woman whose life was as enigmatic as her death.

Mary's Life in New York City's Social Scene

New York City in the 1840s was a place of vibrant contradictions. Streets thrummed with the energy of rapid urbanization, drawing people from every walk of life. Theaters like the Park Theatre and Niblo's Garden became cultural hubs where the city's elite mingled with the working class. Social clubs and salons provided venues for intellectual discourse and networking, each gathering a microcosm of the city's diverse social fabric. Amid this backdrop, Mary Rogers carved out her place, navigating the complexities of a society in flux.

Mary's presence in these social circles was both a testament to her charm and a necessity driven by her ambitions. She formed friendships with individuals from various strata of society: artists, writers, and businessmen who frequented the tobacco shop. These interactions extended beyond mere business transactions; they were opportunities for Mary to engage with the city's cultural life. She attended theater performances and social gatherings, where her eloquence and poise left lasting impressions. Her network included not only loyal customers but also friends who saw in her a blend of intelligence and grace.

Mary's aspirations went beyond her role at the tobacco shop. She harbored dreams of elevating her social standing, seeking opportunities to step out of the shadow of economic hardship. She envisioned a life where she could leverage her charm and intellect to secure a more stable and respected position. To this end, Mary took deliberate steps to improve her social standing. She learned the nuances of social etiquette and engaged in conversations about art, politics, and literature. Her interactions were not just social but strategic, each one a step towards a future she hoped to shape.

The social milieu of New York City placed immense pressure on young women to conform to societal expectations. Mary faced the dual challenge of maintaining her reputation while pursuing her dreams. The societal pressure to marry was ever-present, with young women expected to secure their futures through advantageous marriages. Yet, Mary's ambitions often conflicted with these expectations. She sought independence and respect, aspirations that were not always aligned with the traditional roles prescribed for women of her time. This conflict created a tension that permeated her social interactions and personal decisions.

Mary's life was a constant balancing act, navigating the fine line between personal desire and societal expectations. She attended social events with the hope of meeting influential individuals who could help her achieve her goals, yet she had to ensure that her actions remained within the bounds of propriety. The scrutiny she faced was relentless, with every move analyzed and judged by a society that held women to exacting standards. This pressure to maintain a particular reputation was a burden that Mary carried with grace, even as it weighed heavily on her.

In the bustling social scene of 19th-century New York, Mary Rogers stood as a figure of both fascination and resilience. Her participation in the city's cultural life was not merely a pursuit of enjoyment but a strategic effort to carve out a future that defied the limitations imposed by her circumstances. Her friendships and interactions were a testament to her ability to navigate a complex social landscape, each one contributing to the rich tapestry of her life. As we delve deeper into Mary's story, we will uncover the layers of ambition, struggle, and societal pressure that defined her existence in a rapidly changing world.

The Last Days Before Her Disappearance

In the final days before her disappearance, Mary Rogers' life seemed to follow its usual rhythm, yet subtle shifts hinted at underlying tensions. On July 25, 1841, Mary told her fiancé, Daniel Payne, that she intended to visit her aunt in New Jersey. This was not an unusual statement; Mary often visited relatives and friends outside the city. However, this particular visit would be the last time Daniel saw her alive. Witnesses later confirmed that Mary was seen boarding a ferry to Hoboken, a standard route for those looking to escape the city's heat. Her demeanor during these sightings raised no alarms; she appeared calm and composed, offering no indication that anything was amiss.

As Mary made her way to Hoboken, she interacted with several individuals, each providing a piece of the puzzle that would later confound investigators. One witness reported seeing her with a tall, dark-complexioned man, possibly a naval officer. This sighting added an element of intrigue, as it was unclear whether this man was a friend, a foe, or a stranger. The ferry ride was uneventful, and Mary's presence went largely unnoticed by the other passengers. Yet, the man's identity and his connection to Mary, if any, remained shrouded in mystery.

Mary's last conversations with friends and family revealed little of her inner turmoil. She spoke to her mother about mundane matters, giving no hint of any distress. However, those close to her later recalled minor signs of unease. A few days before her disappearance, Mary had seemed quieter, more introspective. She was known for her lively spirit, so this subtle change did not go unnoticed. Friends mentioned that she had appeared distracted, as if something weighed heavily on her mind. Yet, when pressed, Mary dismissed their concerns, attributing her mood to the summer heat and the pressures of work.

Speculation about Mary's state of mind in those final days is inevitably tinged with the hindsight of tragedy. Some theorized that she might have been grappling with hidden fears or anxieties. The pressures of her public role, combined with the relentless scrutiny she faced, could have taken a toll on her mental well-being. There were whispers that Mary had expressed concerns about a man who had been persistently following her, though these claims were never substantiated. Her interactions, while outwardly normal, may have masked a more profound sense of foreboding.

Testimonies from those who saw Mary in her last days painted a picture of normalcy tinged with underlying tension. Her mother, Phoebe, recalled their final conversation, noting that Mary had seemed preoccupied but not unduly worried. Daniel Payne's recollections were more fragmented, colored by his own grief and guilt. He remembered Mary's affectionate farewell, her promise to return soon. Yet, he also admitted that, in retrospect, there had been an indefinable sadness in her eyes, a fleeting shadow that he could not quite place.

Conflicting reports only deepened the mystery surrounding Mary's disappearance. Some witnesses claimed to have seen her with several men in Hoboken, while others insisted she had been alone. These discrepancies complicated the investigation, offering multiple, often contradictory, narratives. The anonymous letter that surfaced, alleging that Mary had been seen with six men on the day of her disappearance, added another layer of confusion. Each account, while potentially credible, seemed to lead investigators down divergent paths, none of which provided a clear answer.

Unusual occurrences in the days leading up to Mary's disappearance set the stage for the tragedy that would unfold. There were reports of a mysterious man loitering near the tobacco shop, his intentions unclear. Some speculated that Mary had been receiving threatening letters, though no concrete evidence of this was ever found. These unexplained events, coupled with Mary's sudden change in demeanor, hinted at a looming danger that she perhaps sensed but could not escape.

As the sun set on July 25, 1841, Mary Rogers vanished into the folds of history, leaving behind a trail of questions and half-answered clues. Her disappearance was not just the loss of a beloved figure but the beginning of a mystery that would captivate and confound for generations. The days leading up to her disappearance were filled with mundane interactions and subtle signs of unease, a blend of normalcy and tension that set the stage for the enigma that was to come. Mary's final days, though ordinary in many respects, were marked by an undercurrent of uncertainty, foreshadowing the tragic fate that awaited her.

CHAPTER 2

THE DAY SHE DISAPPEARED

The Timeline of July 25, 1841

July 25, 1841, began as many summer days in New York City did, with the early morning light filtering through the dense haze of the bustling metropolis. Mary Rogers' day started with a routine that was both familiar and comforting. Rising early, she prepared herself for the day ahead, meticulously dressing in a way that balanced modesty with the undeniable charm that had earned her the nickname "Beautiful Cigar Girl." She exchanged a few words with her mother, Phoebe, over breakfast, discussing her plans to visit her aunt in New Jersey. This plan, though ordinary, would mark the beginning of her final journey, a journey that many of us can relate to in our own lives.

As the morning progressed, Mary left her family's boarding house and made her way through the crowded streets that had become a second home to her. The sights and sounds of the city were both a comfort and a reminder of the ever-present dangers that lurked in the shadows. She arrived at the tobacco shop where she worked, engaging in her usual tasks with the same grace and efficiency that had become her hallmark. Customers came and went, each interaction a blend of business and the subtle charm that Mary exuded effortlessly.

By late morning, Mary had completed her duties at the shop and was seen preparing for her trip to Hoboken. She gathered her belongings and made her way to the ferry terminal, a familiar route for those seeking a brief respite from the city's heat. It was here that several witnesses last saw her, her presence noted by the regular commuters who shared the ferry ride with her. The ferry ride itself was uneventful, a brief journey across the river that offered a moment of quiet reflection amidst the hustle and bustle of daily life.

As Mary disembarked in Hoboken, the day took on a mysterious air. Witnesses reported seeing her with a tall, dark-complexioned man, a figure whose identity remains shrouded in speculation. Some described him as a naval officer, while others suggested he was a stranger who had taken an unusual interest in Mary. The precise nature of their interaction is lost to history, but it added a layer of intrigue to an already enigmatic day.

Throughout the afternoon, Mary's movements became increasingly difficult to trace as witnesses reported conflicting sightings-some claiming she visited a local tavern, others insisting she was walking along the waterfront-adding layers of uncertainty that deepen the intrigue surrounding her final hours.

As evening approached, the sightings of Mary became even more sporadic. The last confirmed sighting placed her near Castle Point, a secluded area that offered a stark contrast to the lively streets of New York City. Here, she was reportedly seen in the company of several men, their rough appearance raising suspicions among those who observed them. This sighting would later become a focal point in the investigation, raising questions about the nature of her interactions and the circumstances that led to her tragic end.

The search for Mary Rogers began almost immediately after her disappearance, and for those closest to her, it was a harrowing experience. Daniel Payne, her fiancé, was consumed by worry, pacing the streets and questioning anyone who might have seen her. Each passing hour intensified his fear, and by the second day, his desperation had turned into frantic disbelief. John Anderson, the tobacco shop owner, was equally distraught. His mind raced with troubling thoughts of what might have befallen the young woman who had been such a central figure in his life and business. The weight of their emotions was palpable as they combed the streets and ferry terminals, their faces etched with dread. Both men were haunted by the possibility that she had met with foul play, and the lack of answers further fueled their anguish, each lead evaporating like mist in the summer heat.

The final hours of Mary's life remain a blend of fact and speculation. Witnesses described her as calm and composed, yet subtle signs of unease hinted at deeper turmoil. Her interactions, while seemingly ordinary, carried an undercurrent of tension that only became apparent in hindsight. The environment she moved through, from the bustling ferry terminal to the quiet seclusion of Castle Point, mirrored the duality of her public persona and private fears.

The timeline of Mary Rogers' disappearance is marked by gaps and inconsistencies that have fueled speculation for generations. Some accounts suggest she disappeared shortly after she arrived in Hoboken, while others insist she was seen well into the evening. These discrepancies have created a labyrinth of conflicting narratives, each offering a different perspective on her final moments. The absence of concrete evidence has only deepened the mystery, leaving investigators and amateur sleuths alike to piece together the fragments of that fateful day. This mystery continues to intrigue us to this day.

Modern forensic techniques, if available at the time, might have provided clarity to the enigma of Mary's disappearance. DNA analysis, advanced imaging, and psychological profiling could have offered insights into the identity of her companions and the nature of her final interactions. Yet, in the absence of such tools, the investigation relied heavily on witness testimonies and the limited forensic methods of the era. These testimonies, often conflicting and influenced by personal biases, and the lack of sophisticated forensic tools made the investigation of Mary's disappearance a challenging and complex task.

The day Mary Rogers disappeared is a haunting chapter in the annals of New York City's history, not only for her routine and interactions but also for how her case reflected societal tensions and cultural norms of 19th-century America, making it a significant chapter in our history.

Witness Accounts and Last Sightings

The morning of July 25, 1841, was filled with the usual hustle and bustle, but for those who encountered Mary Rogers, it was a day that would be etched into their memories forever. Friends and family members provided accounts that painted a picture of her last known activities. Her mother, Phoebe, recalled Mary leaving their boarding house with a calm demeanor, dressed in her usual modest attire. Daniel Payne, her fiancé, recounted their brief conversation where Mary mentioned her plan to visit her aunt. He noted nothing unusual in her behavior, only a sense of routine that gave no hint of the tragedy to come. The disappearance of Mary also had a profound impact on her community, sparking fear and suspicion among the residents of New York City and leading to a public outcry for increased safety measures.

As Mary made her way to the ferry terminal, she interacted with several passersby, each providing snippets of her journey. A shopkeeper near the terminal remembered selling her a small bundle of goods, noting her polite but distant manner. Another witness, a young woman who frequently traveled the same route, described Mary as somewhat preoccupied but still composed. These early sightings established a pattern of normalcy, yet each interaction carried an undercurrent of something unspoken, a subtle tension that only became significant in hindsight.

Among the most compelling accounts came from strangers who observed Mary during her ferry ride to Hoboken. A fellow passenger, a middle-aged man with a keen eye for detail, provided a vivid description of Mary standing by the railing, gazing out at the water with a thoughtful expression. He noted her attire, a simple dress that was both practical and elegant, and her demeanor, which seemed contemplative yet untroubled. Another passenger, a woman traveling with her children, remembered Mary's kind smile when one of the children bumped into her, a small gesture that highlighted her warm personality.

As the day progressed, Mary's movements became more fragmented, with sightings reported from various parts of Hoboken. A tavern owner recalled seeing her briefly enter his establishment, her presence causing a stir among the patrons. He described her as polite but reserved, declining hospitality. Another witness, a dockworker, saw her walking along the waterfront, her pace unhurried and her expression unreadable. These sightings, while disparate, formed a mosaic of her final hours, each piece adding to the complexity of her disappearance.

The credibility of these witnesses varied, influenced by their relationships with Mary and their own biases. Friends and family members, deeply affected by her loss, provided accounts that were consistent but tinged with personal grief. Strangers, on the other hand, offered observations that were more detached but occasionally inconsistent. Some reports described Mary's demeanor as calm and composed, while others described her as distracted or anxious. These conflicting descriptions created a web of uncertainty, complicating the efforts to piece together her final movements.

Key sightings emerged as particularly significant in understanding Mary's disappearance. One of the last confirmed sightings came from a local shopkeeper who saw her near Castle Point in the late afternoon. He described her as being in the company of a tall, dark-complexioned man, a detail that would later become central to the investigation. The shopkeeper's account was detailed, noting Mary's attire and the man's distinctive features, but it also raised questions about the nature of their interaction. Was he a friend, an acquaintance, or someone with more sinister intentions?

Other witnesses provided accounts that conflicted with this narrative, describing Mary as being alone or in the company of different individuals. A fisherman along the riverbank claimed to have seen her walking alone, her steps purposeful but her expression somber. Another witness, a resident, insisted a group of men had accompanied her, their rough demeanor contrasting sharply with her elegance. These discrepancies, while frustrating for investigators, highlighted the challenges of relying on eyewitness testimonies, each colored by personal perception and memory.

The disappearance of Mary Rogers cast a shadow over the entire city. Neighbors who had once moved about their daily routines without fear now whispered anxiously about the possibility of danger lurking in every corner. Hoboken residents who had seen her that day began to second-guess their own memories, questioning whether they had overlooked any crucial detail. As the search expanded, the community banded together, driven by a shared sense of concern. Strangers became allies, offering information and resources to aid in the search. There was a collective hope that finding Mary would restore order, but as each day passed without answers, that hope slowly gave way to an unsettling realization that something far more sinister had occurred. The sense of safety that many had taken for granted dissolved, replaced by an undercurrent of fear and suspicion.

The varying accounts of Mary's clothing and behavior added another layer of complexity. Some witnesses described her dress as light-colored and straightforward, while others insisted it was darker and more ornate. Her demeanor, too, was a subject of debate: was she calm and composed, or did she exude an air of unease? These differing descriptions created a tapestry of uncertainty, each thread contributing to the larger mystery of Mary's final day.

The media played an outsized role in shaping the public's perception of Mary's disappearance. Newspapers, eager to exploit the drama of her case, sensationalized every detail. The *New York Sun* and *New York Herald* plastered Mary's image across their front pages, painting her as a tragic, angelic figure caught in the dangers of city life. Headlines speculated wildly about possible kidnappings, secret lovers, and foul play. Each story seemed to outdo the last, stoking public hysteria. These sensational reports did more than inform; they shaped the narrative, pushing law enforcement to act quickly under public pressure. In many ways, the frenzied media coverage set the tone for how Mary's case would be remembered: not simply as a tragic mystery but as one of the earliest instances of media-driven spectacle, echoing the sensationalism seen in modern-day cases.

The conflicting reports and unexplained absences in the timeline of Mary Rogers' disappearance have fueled speculation and intrigue for generations. Each account, whether from friends, family, or strangers, offers a glimpse into her last known moments, yet none provide the definitive answers that could unravel the enigma of her fate. The day she disappeared is a chapter filled with shadows and half-truths, a puzzle that remains tantalizingly incomplete.

The Social and Cultural Context of the Time

In 1841, New York City was a hub of transformation. Its population was exploding, driven by waves of immigration and the promise of opportunity. The city's streets were filled with a mix of languages and cultures, creating a dynamic but often chaotic environment. This rapid urbanization brought both progress and challenges. The city's social fabric was complex, marked by stark contrasts between the wealthy elite and the struggling working class.

Crime was a constant concern, and public fear was palpable. Murders, thefts, and assaults were common, and sensational cases like that of Helen Jewett, a prostitute murdered in 1836, had already gripped the public imagination. Law enforcement was rudimentary, relying on a patchwork of night watchmen and constables who were often ill-equipped and undertrained. The lack of a professional police force meant crime was seen as an ever-present threat, further heightening the anxiety of city life.

The media played a significant role in shaping public perception of crime. The penny press, with its affordable and sensationalized newspapers, fed the public's hunger for scandal and intrigue. Headlines were crafted to capture attention, often at the expense of accuracy. Mary Rogers' disappearance and subsequent murder provided ample fodder for these publications. Newspapers like the New York Sun and the New York Herald ran stories that blurred the lines between fact and fiction, each trying to outdo the other with more lurid details.

Specific articles about Mary's case painted her as a tragic figure, a young woman caught in the dangerous web of city life. These stories were not just reports; they were narratives that captivated readers, making Mary a household name. The media's influence extended beyond just informing the public; it shaped the investigation itself, with law enforcement feeling the pressure to solve the case quickly to appease a restless populace.

Urban dynamics were changing rapidly, impacting social interactions and public safety. Neighborhoods were developing at a breakneck pace, often without adequate infrastructure or planning. This haphazard growth created pockets of prosperity alongside areas of extreme poverty, each with its own unique challenges. Public spaces like parks and markets were bustling with activity, but they were also hotspots for crime. Women, in particular, faced heightened risks as they navigated these urban landscapes. The societal expectation for women to maintain a veneer of modesty and propriety often left them vulnerable, as venturing out alone was both a necessity and a peril.

Rapid urbanization also led to the rise of social spaces where people from different backgrounds could interact. Theaters, salons, and social clubs became melting pots of ideas and influences, but they also served as stages for the drama of everyday life. For women like Mary, these spaces provided a rare opportunity to engage with the world beyond the confines of domesticity. However, this visibility came with its own set of dangers, as public life was fraught with scrutiny and judgment.

A combination of fear and fascination shaped public attitudes towards crime. People were drawn to the macabre details of violent acts, yet they were also deeply concerned about their own safety. The media capitalized on this duality, providing a steady stream of crime stories that both entertained and alarmed. The case of Mary Rogers was a perfect example of this phenomenon. Her murder was not just a crime; it was a narrative that reflected the anxieties and curiosities of the time.

Law enforcement practices of the era were often reactive rather than proactive. The lack of modern forensic techniques meant that investigations relied heavily on witness testimonies and rudimentary evidence collection. This approach was fraught with challenges, as the chaotic urban environment often contaminated crime scenes and muddied the waters of justice. The societal response to crime was similarly fragmented, with communities banding together for protection while also demanding more from their leaders.

The role of women in society was undergoing a subtle but significant shift. The market revolution and the Second Great Awakening began to change how women were perceived and what was expected of them. While the ideal of the "separate spheres" doctrine still held sway, with men occupying the public domain and women the private, there were emerging opportunities for women to assert their influence. This period saw the rise of female social reformers and activists who began to challenge the status quo, advocating for greater rights and protections.

Mary Rogers' life and death must be viewed against this backdrop of social change and cultural tension. Her role as a "Beautiful Cigar Girl" broke the mold of what was acceptable for women, making her both a symbol of change and a target of societal judgment. The public's fascination with her, fueled by the media, reflected the broader anxieties and aspirations of a city in flux. Her murder, unsolved and enigmatic, remains a poignant reminder of the complexities and contradictions of 19th-century New York.

Gender Expectations and Mary's Public Life

In 1841, societal norms for women were rigid and unforgiving. Women were expected to embody the virtues of purity, piety, and domesticity. The "Cult of True Womanhood" held that a woman's sphere was her home and that her primary roles were those of wife and mother. Public life was primarily reserved for men, and any deviation from these prescribed roles often led to social ostracism. Women who stepped outside these boundaries faced intense scrutiny and judgment. This cultural backdrop profoundly influenced Mary Rogers' life, both publicly and privately.

Mary's public persona as the "Beautiful Cigar Girl" placed her in direct conflict with these societal norms. Working in a tobacco shop, interacting with a predominantly male clientele, and becoming a minor celebrity in her own right, she was an anomaly in a world that preferred women to remain unseen and unheard. Her beauty and charm made her a subject of fascination, but this visibility came with its own set of challenges. Social pressures and moral expectations weighed heavily on her as she struggled to balance her ambitions with the restrictive roles imposed on her gender.

Navigating these societal expectations was a delicate act for Mary. In her public role, she exuded confidence and grace, engaging customers and maintaining professionalism. Yet, this public persona often masked the conflicts she faced in her private life. Instances of defiance were subtle but significant. By taking on a job that put her in the public eye, Mary challenged the norms that confined women to the domestic sphere. However, she also had to conform in specific ways to avoid scandal and maintain her reputation. Her relationship with Daniel Payne, her fiancé, reflected this delicate balance. While she sought independence through her work, she also adhered to societal expectations of marriage and propriety.

Gender biases played a significant role in the investigation into Mary's disappearance and subsequent murder. The initial focus was heavily skewed towards her personal life and relationships rather than a broader examination of potential suspects or motives. Stereotypes about her character influenced public and media perceptions. As a woman in a visible role, Mary was often viewed through a lens of suspicion and moral judgment. Assumptions about her behavior and associations colored the investigation, diverting attention from other critical leads.

The intense public and media scrutiny of Mary's life was inescapable. Newspapers and periodicals were quick to cast her as either a tragic victim or a cautionary tale. Her beauty and social status made her a compelling figure for sensational journalism, but this portrayal often lacked nuance and depth. The media's focus on her appearance and personal life overshadowed the more complex aspects of her character and the circumstances of her death. This gendered attention not only influenced public opinion but also shaped the investigative efforts, creating a narrative that was as much about societal fears and fascinations as it was about finding justice for Mary.

The portrayal of Mary in the media was a double-edged sword. On one hand, it kept her case in the public eye, ensuring that it remained a topic of discussion and debate. On the other hand, it reduced her to a symbol, stripping away the complexities of her life and reducing her to a mere archetype. She was simultaneously idolized and vilified, her story used to reinforce or challenge existing moral frameworks, depending on the agenda of the storyteller. This public fascination with her beauty and social status was both a boon and a burden, shaping the investigation in ways that were often unhelpful and, at times, even detrimental.

As we continue this exploration of Mary Rogers' life and death, it is crucial to remember the societal context in which she lived. The gender expectations of the time were not just background details; they were active forces that shaped every aspect of her existence. From her public role to the investigation of her murder, Mary's story is deeply intertwined with the cultural and social dynamics of 19th-century America. Understanding these dynamics is key to unraveling the mystery surrounding her and shedding light on the broader implications of her tragic fate.

CHAPTER 3

THE DISCOVERY OF MARY ROGERS' BODY

The Search Efforts Begin

July 28, 1841, began as another sweltering summer day in New York City, but for Mary Rogers' family and friends, it marked the start of a case that would grip the nation. Mary had been missing for three days, and the growing anxiety underscored the case's societal impact. Phoebe Rogers, her mother, was the first to sense that something was terribly wrong, as the absence of Mary's laughter and footsteps in their boarding house on Nassau Street deepened her fears. She reached out to friends and acquaintances, hoping someone had seen or heard from Mary. Her concern quickly spread, igniting a city-wide search that would become a symbol of 19th-century urban crime and social concern.

Daniel Payne, Mary's fiancé, was equally frantic. He retraced Mary's known steps, speaking to anyone who might have seen her. His desperation drove him to the police, urging them to take swift action. The authorities, initially slow and under-resourced, began to recognize the gravity of the situation as media coverage of Mary's disappearance intensified. The police force at the time lacked modern resources and procedures, making their efforts more difficult. Nevertheless, they mobilized, driven by public pressure and the growing concern from Mary's loved ones, highlighting the investigative limitations of the era.

The search for Mary Rogers was a community effort, with everyone from local shopkeepers to concerned neighbors joining in. The areas searched were extensive, covering the parks, streets, and waterfronts of both New York and Hoboken. Volunteers scoured the bustling streets where Mary was last seen, while others ventured into the city's quieter, more treacherous parts. The waterfront, with its rocky terrain and strong currents, posed significant difficulties. The oppressive summer heat added to their hardships, illustrating the community's collective resolve to find her and the societal importance placed on such cases in the 19th century.

John Anderson, Mary's employer at the tobacco shop, was deeply involved in the search. Known for his business acumen, Anderson used his resources to organize search teams and coordinate efforts across the city. He reached out to his extensive network of clients and associates, urging them to help find Mary. Daniel Payne, though consumed with fear and guilt, was relentless in his efforts. His determination was evident as he combed through every possible lead, refusing to rest until Mary was found. Their dedication was mirrored by the local community, with neighbors and volunteers tirelessly searching day and night.

As hours turned into days, the urgency to find Mary grew. The emotional toll on her family and friends was devastating. Phoebe Rogers, normally a pillar of strength, found herself overwhelmed by waves of despair and hope. Each passing moment without news felt like an eternity, amplifying her anguish. Daniel Payne's anxiety turned to visible distress, his typically composed demeanor shattered by the weight of uncertainty. Their anguish was shared by the searchers, who felt the mounting pressure to find Mary and bring an end to the nightmare that had engulfed the community.

The authorities, too, felt the strain. The mounting pressure from the public and the media intensified their efforts. Every lead, no matter how tenuous, was pursued with vigor. Police officers, often overworked and underpaid, pushed themselves to the limit, driven by the urgency of the case and the demands of a city on edge. The search became a race against time, with everyone involved acutely aware that each passing hour diminished the chances of finding Mary alive.

The growing desperation was evident on the searchers' faces, each marked by fatigue and determination. The emotional toll was visible in their strained expressions and weary movements. Yet, despite the exhaustion, the community's resolve remained unbroken. The hope of finding Mary and bringing her back to her family fueled their relentless pursuit. This collective effort, born of love and concern, highlighted the deep bond of community and the lengths people would go to protect one of their own.

As the sun set on July 28, the sense of urgency reached its peak. The searchers, driven by a mix of hope and dread, continued their efforts into the night. The city, normally alive with the sounds of evening activities, seemed to hold its breath, waiting for news. The discovery of Mary Rogers' body, when it finally came, would shatter the fragile hope that had sustained the searchers and cast a long shadow over the city, marking the beginning of a mystery that would captivate and confound for generations.

Finding Mary: The Grim Discovery on the Hudson

On July 28, 1841, the grim discovery of Mary Rogers' body was made by two local boys, Henry Mallin and James M. Boullard, who were exploring the area near Sybil's Cave along the Hudson River. They were initially drawn to the location by the unusual sight of a bundle floating near the shoreline. As they approached, the outline of a woman's body became horrifyingly clear. At first, they were struck by disbelief, their innocent day of exploration turning into a scene from a nightmare. Their initial reactions were a mix of shock and fear, quickly transforming into a frantic call for help.

The emotional toll on the two young boys, Henry Mallin and James M. Boullard, was immediate and profound. What began as a carefree day of exploration along the Hudson turned into a traumatic discovery that would haunt them for the rest of their lives. Their initial reactions of shock quickly gave way to panic as they grappled with the horrific reality of finding a lifeless body. For weeks after, nightmares plagued the boys, their innocence shattered by the gruesome scene they had unwittingly stumbled upon. The weight of their discovery cast a long shadow over their lives, marking them as unwilling participants in one of the city's darkest moments.

The exact location where Mary's body was found added a macabre twist to the discovery. Sybil's Cave, a man-made grotto created in 1832 to access a natural spring, had become a popular local attraction. It was here, amidst the picturesque setting, that the stark reality of Mary's fate was revealed. Her body lay partly submerged in the water, the natural beauty of the cave juxtaposed against the horror of her death. The boys' cries soon attracted a crowd, turning the serene spot into a chaotic scene filled with murmurs of disbelief and grief.

The condition of Mary Rogers' body told a story of violence and struggle. She was found with visible injuries that indicated a brutal assault. Her clothing was disheveled, and there were clear signs of a physical battle. The coroner later noted evidence of strangulation, along with multiple bruises and lacerations on her body. These injuries suggested that Mary had fought fiercely against her attacker. The position of her body, lying face up with her arms outstretched, hinted at the desperation of her final moments. The state of decomposition indicated that she had been dead for several days, aligning with the timeline of her disappearance on July 25.

The discovery site quickly became a hive of activity as law enforcement arrived to secure the area. The initial handling of the crime scene reflected the limitations of the era's investigative practices. The boys who discovered Mary's body had already disturbed the scene, driven by their panic and the need to summon help. When the authorities arrived, they faced the challenge of preserving as much evidence as possible amidst the growing crowd. Officers cordoned off the area, pushing back onlookers and trying to maintain order. The immediate actions taken by the discoverers, though well-intentioned, had already compromised crucial forensic evidence.

The retrieval of Mary's body from the river was carried out with a somber efficiency. Law enforcement officials, assisted by local volunteers, used a makeshift stretcher to lift her body from the water, taking care to avoid further damage. The process was painstaking, with each movement carefully coordinated to preserve the integrity of the evidence. The body was then transported to the coroner's office for a more thorough examination. The journey from the riverside to the medical examiner's office was a somber procession marked by the respectful silence of those involved. Each step in the retrieval process was a reminder of the gravity of the crime and the importance of finding justice for Mary.

As Mary's body was transported, the mood shifted from the initial shock of discovery to a grim determination. The coroner's examination would later confirm the cause of death as strangulation, alongside evidence of a brutal beating and possible sexual assault. These findings painted a harrowing picture of Mary's final moments, underscoring the violence she had endured. The meticulous documentation of her injuries provided vital clues, yet the absence of advanced forensic techniques left many questions unanswered.

SYBIL'S CAVE, AT HOBOKEN, N. J.

The discovery of Mary Rogers' body marked a turning point in the investigation, transforming the search for a missing woman into a hunt for a murderer. The serene setting of Sybil's Cave, once a place of leisure, became a symbol of tragedy. The immediate actions of the community, from the boys who stumbled upon her body to the officers who secured the scene, reflected a collective resolve to uncover the truth. The retrieval and transport of her body were carried out with a somber respect, each step a testament to the gravity of the crime and the enduring impact of Mary's untimely death.

Public Reaction and Media Frenzy

The discovery of Mary Rogers' body sent shockwaves through New York City. News of the grisly find spread like wildfire, pulling people from their daily routines into a communal state of horror and fascination. Crowds gathered near Sybil's Cave, their faces etched with a mix of curiosity and dread. Conversations buzzed with speculation, each person eager to share their theories or recount the latest rumor. The air was thick with tension, punctuated by the occasional gasp or murmur of disbelief. For many, the tragedy felt personal, as if a member of their own family had been lost.

The media seized upon the discovery of Mary's body with unparalleled fervor, turning a tragedy into a spectacle. Newspapers painted vivid, often exaggerated, portraits of the scene at Sybil's Cave, feeding the public's insatiable hunger for details. Sensational headlines screamed from the front pages, each story more lurid than the last. These reports not only stoked public outrage but also shaped the course of the investigation. The pressure from the press pushed law enforcement to act swiftly, often at the expense of thoroughness. Speculation in the papers blurred the line between fact and fiction, creating a narrative that would haunt the investigation and public discourse for months to come.

The community's emotional responses were intense and immediate. Mothers clutched their children a little tighter, haunted by the thought that it could have been their daughter found in the Hudson. Men, often stoic in their daily lives, found themselves grappling with helplessness and anger. The streets, generally filled with the cacophony of everyday life, were subdued, the usual clamor replaced by hushed conversations and somber faces. In homes and taverns, people gathered to discuss the news, each retelling of the discovery adding layers of emotion and conjecture.

Newspapers seized upon the story with a fervor that bordered on mania. The sensational headlines screamed from the front pages, each one more lurid than the last. "The Beautiful Cigar Girl Found Dead!" blared one paper, while another declared, "Murder Most Foul: The Mystery of Mary Rogers." The New York Sun and the New York Herald led the charge, their reporters weaving narratives that captivated and horrified in equal measure. Articles were filled with vivid descriptions of Mary's body, the circumstances of her death, and speculative theories about her killer. The press, ever eager to outdo each other, did not shy away from dramatizing every detail, turning Mary's tragedy into a public spectacle.

Prominent newspapers played a significant role in shaping the narrative. Their coverage was a blend of fact, conjecture, and outright fiction, each edition designed to capture the public's attention and sell more copies. Reporters interviewed anyone remotely connected to the case, from Mary's coworkers to casual acquaintances, whose statements were often twisted to fit the salacious tone of the story. This relentless media coverage amplified the public's horror and fascination, creating an atmosphere where fact and fiction became indistinguishable.

For Mary's family, the media frenzy was a double-edged sword. On one hand, it ensured that her case remained in the public eye, increasing the pressure on authorities to find her killer. On the other hand, it invaded their privacy, turning their personal grief into public consumption. Phoebe Rogers, already devastated by the loss of her daughter, found herself besieged by reporters eager for a quote or a photograph. Her sorrow was laid bare for the world to see, each tear and tremor captured and broadcast for the masses. Daniel Payne, too, was not spared. His anguish was dissected in print, his every move scrutinized and reported with little regard for his emotional state.

The intrusion into their private lives added another layer of torment. Statements from family members were often taken out of context, and their grief was used to fuel the media's sensational narratives. Interviews were conducted in the most vulnerable moments, and the rawness of their pain lay bare for readers who devoured each new detail. This relentless pursuit of the story left Mary's family feeling exposed and violated; their personal tragedy turned into a public spectacle.

The discovery of Mary's body also sparked broader societal debates. Public discussions about urban safety and crime became more urgent, with many questioning the effectiveness of the city's law enforcement. The tragic end of the "Beautiful Cigar Girl" highlighted the dangers that lurked in the rapidly growing metropolis, sparking calls for reform and better protection for women. Public meetings were held, and letters to the editor filled newspaper pages, each a testament to the collective anxiety and desire for change. The case became a catalyst for examining broader issues of safety and justice in New York City, influencing local policies and public sentiment that would be felt for years to come.

The discovery of Mary Rogers' body also forced New York City to confront uncomfortable truths about the vulnerabilities women faced in urban environments. Her death sparked public outcry for improved safety measures, particularly for women who, like Mary, navigated the city's streets both in public and in their professional lives. Discussions about policing and public order took on new urgency as people called for more protections in the rapidly expanding city. The case highlighted the dangers of a society that placed women in the public eye while offering little in the way of safety, prompting a conversation about reforms to reshape the city's approach to crime prevention.

The public's response to Mary's murder was a mix of fear, anger, and a desperate need for justice. The community's horror at the crime translated into a demand for action, putting immense pressure on the authorities to solve the case. This case, with its blend of beauty, violence, and mystery, tapped into the deepest fears and fascinations of the time, making it a defining moment in the city's history. The societal implications were profound, touching on issues of gender, safety, and the power of the media, each thread weaving into the complex tapestry of Mary Rogers' life and death.

Initial Theories and Suspicions

In the immediate aftermath of Mary Rogers' body being found, theories about her murder began to swirl, each more speculative than the last. Initial suspicions ranged from personal vendettas to random acts of violence. Some believed that jealousy or revenge might have driven someone close to Mary to commit the heinous act. Others speculated that she had fallen victim to a stranger or a gang, given the rising crime rates in New York City. These theories were fueled by the brutal nature of her death and the mysterious circumstances surrounding her disappearance.

Daniel Payne, Mary's fiancé, was one of the early suspects. His close relationship with Mary made him a focal point for investigators. Payne's visible distress and erratic behavior following her disappearance raised eyebrows. He had an alibi, but his emotional turmoil and subsequent suicide only deepened suspicions. Payne's profile was that of a man deeply in love, yet his actions in the wake of Mary's death seemed to suggest a level of guilt or at least an overwhelming sense of responsibility.

John Anderson, Mary's employer at the tobacco shop, was another figure of interest. Anderson had a reputation for being both charming and ambitious. His close professional relationship with Mary made him a subject of scrutiny. Some speculated that Anderson might have had a personal interest in Mary beyond a professional one. Theories suggested that jealousy or unrequited affection could have driven him to commit the crime. Despite his public efforts to find Mary, whispers about his potential involvement lingered.

Other suspects emerged from the shadows of the city's underbelly. The theory of gang involvement was particularly compelling, given the violent nature of Mary's death. Some believed that she had been targeted by a local gang, either as a random act of violence or as part of a broader criminal agenda. This theory was supported by accounts of rough-looking men seen near the location where her body was found. The idea that Mary had been caught in a web of urban crime resonated with a public already anxious about the safety of their city.

Public and media speculation ran rampant, often without a shred of concrete evidence. Rumors and gossip became the currency of the day, with each new theory adding fuel to the fire. Newspapers printed sensational stories that ranged from plausible to absurd, each one designed to captivate readers and sell more copies. The media frenzy blurred the lines between fact and fiction, making it difficult for investigators to separate credible leads from wild speculation. This atmosphere of conjecture and sensationalism only complicated the investigation.

The early investigative efforts were a mix of determination and missteps. Authorities interviewed a slew of witnesses, from Mary's friends and family to casual acquaintances and strangers who claimed to have seen her. The methods used to gather evidence were rudimentary by today's standards, relying heavily on testimonies and physical evidence that was often contaminated or incomplete. Investigators faced the challenge of sifting through conflicting accounts and unreliable witnesses, each one adding a piece to a puzzle that refused to come together.

Missteps were inevitable in such a high-pressure investigation. The initial handling of the crime scene, with its contamination by onlookers and the media, hindered the collection of vital evidence. Crucial leads were sometimes overlooked or dismissed in the rush to find quick answers. Yet, there were also moments of success. The discovery of Mary's personal items in a wooded area near the river provided critical clues. These items, though found weeks after her body, offered insights into the possible timeline and location of her death.

Despite the challenges, the urgency to solve Mary Rogers' murder drove the investigation forward. Each theory, suspect, and piece of evidence was meticulously examined, even as the pressure from the public and media mounted. The early stages of the investigation set the stage for a complex and often frustrating pursuit of justice. As the case unfolded, the blend of fact, fiction, and relentless speculation painted a vivid yet fragmented picture of a city grappling with one of its most haunting mysteries. The search for Mary's killer would continue to captivate and confound, leaving an indelible mark on the cultural and historical landscape of New York City.

CHAPTER 4

THE MEDIA STORM

The Role of the Penny Press

MARY ROGERS, THE CIGAR GIRL.
Murdered at Hoboken, July 25, 1841.

The streets of New York City were abuzz with a mix of excitement and trepidation as news of Mary Rogers' murder spread. It was an era when newspapers had begun to shape the very fabric of society, and few innovations were as influential as the penny press. Emerging in the 1830s, these inexpensive, widely accessible newspapers transformed the media landscape and public opinion. The penny press catered to an audience that traditional, more expensive publications had long overlooked. Before this shift, newspapers were primarily the domain of upper-class, urban, professional males. But with the advent of the penny press, information became democratized, reaching the working class and sparking a revolution in how news was consumed.

The rise of the penny press marked a significant departure from previous media practices. Newspapers like the New York Sun and the New York Herald were at the forefront of this movement, pioneering a new approach to journalism that relied heavily on sensationalism and human interest stories. These papers were sold for just a penny, making them affordable to the masses. The business model was simple yet effective: low-cost production coupled with high circulation goals. This approach necessitated a focus on eye-catching headlines and dramatic stories that would captivate readers and boost sales.

Understanding the psychological nuances of individuals like Daniel Payne or John Anderson allows for a more layered interpretation of historical crimes. In modern investigations, applying insights from psychology and criminology can lead to more accurate profiling of suspects and witnesses. Psychological complexity is vital in understanding how trauma and societal expectations can influence actions and decisions. By recognizing these factors in both historical and contemporary cases, we can develop a more empathetic and comprehensive understanding of the human behaviors that play out in criminal investigations.

The readership of the penny press was primarily working-class individuals seeking affordable news and entertainment. This audience had a voracious appetite for stories that reflected their own lives and struggles. Crime, scandal, and human-interest stories were particularly popular, as they offered both a sense of escapism and a mirror of readers' own experiences. The penny press capitalized on this interest, filling their pages with tales of intrigue and sensationalism that kept readers coming back for more.

Mary Rogers' murder was a perfect story for the penny press. It had all the elements that captivated their readers: a beautiful young woman, a mysterious disappearance, and a grisly murder. The newspapers wasted no time in turning Mary's tragic fate into a front-page sensation. Articles about her death were filled with lurid details and speculative theories, each more dramatic than the last. The coverage was relentless, with newspapers vying to outdo each other in their portrayal of the crime. The New York Sun, in particular, capitalized on the public's fascination with Mary Rogers, running numerous stories that sensationalized every aspect of her life and death.

The penny press did more than report the facts; it magnified the details in ways that blurred the line between reporting and entertainment. Headlines were crafted not just to inform but to captivate, using phrases like "tragic beauty" and "mysterious stranger" to draw readers in. Dramatic language was often employed to exaggerate certain aspects of the case; descriptions of Mary Rogers usually focused on her physical appearance, making her beauty central to the narrative. The New York Herald, for example, published speculative pieces that went beyond the evidence, suggesting lurid details about her potential assailants. Newspapers often included fictionalized or speculative accounts of the crime, making it hard for readers to distinguish fact from fiction.

The impact of this coverage was immediate and profound. Newspaper sales skyrocketed as the public clamored for the latest updates on the case. The murder of Mary Rogers became a daily topic of conversation, not just in New York but across the country. The penny press had succeeded in turning a personal tragedy into a public spectacle, manipulating public sentiment and potentially influencing the direction of the investigation. The sensationalism that characterized the coverage of Mary's murder was not just about selling papers; it was about shaping the narrative and, by extension, the public's perception of the crime.

The influence of the penny press extended beyond just the dissemination of news. It played a crucial role in shaping public opinion and societal norms. By focusing on stories that resonated with their readers, these newspapers helped to elevate issues that might otherwise have been overlooked. The case of Mary Rogers, for instance, highlighted concerns about urban safety and the vulnerabilities women face. The relentless coverage brought these issues to the forefront of public discourse, forcing both the authorities and the public to confront uncomfortable truths about their city. This role in shaping public opinion is a significant aspect of the penny press's influence that should not be underestimated.

However, the penny press was not without its critics. The sensationalism and lack of journalistic integrity that often characterized these publications drew condemnation from more traditional media outlets and public figures. Critics argued that the penny press prioritized profit over truth, manipulating facts to create more compelling stories. This critique was not without merit, as the coverage of Mary Rogers' murder often blurred the lines between fact and fiction, creating a narrative that was as much about entertainment as it was about informing the public. This distinction between fact and fiction is a key aspect of the penny press's influence that should be carefully considered.

The legacy of the penny press is complex. On one hand, it democratized access to information, giving voice to the working class and bringing important issues to light. On the other hand, it set a precedent for sensationalism in journalism, a trend that continues to influence media practices today. The murder of Mary Rogers is a case study in the power and pitfalls of the penny press, illustrating both its ability to engage and inform the public and its potential to distort and sensationalize the truth. This potential for distortion and the ethical concerns it raises are key aspects of the penny press's influence that should not be overlooked.

As you navigate the story of Mary Rogers, it's essential to understand the role that the penny press played in shaping the narrative. The newspapers of the time were not just passive observers; they were active participants in the unfolding drama, shaping public perception and potentially the course of the investigation. Their coverage of Mary's murder is a testament to the enduring power of the media to captivate, inform, and sometimes mislead, a power that remains as relevant today as it was in the 19th century.

Sensational Headlines and Public Outrage

As news of Mary Rogers' murder spread, newspapers vied to capture the public's attention with sensational headlines designed to evoke shock and curiosity. "The Beautiful Cigar Girl Found Dead!" screamed one front page, while another declared, "Murder Most Foul: The Mystery of Mary Rogers." These headlines, much like modern clickbait, skewed public opinion and directed the investigation down various paths. The aim was precise: to attract as many readers as possible by capitalizing on the tragedy. Words like "beautiful," "murder," and "mystery" were not just descriptive; they were carefully chosen to stir emotions and draw readers into the unfolding drama.

The language and imagery used in these headlines were crafted with precision. Descriptive words like "beautiful" humanized Mary and made her more relatable, while "murder" and "mystery" added a layer of intrigue and urgency. This combination was irresistible to readers, pulling them into a narrative that was both thrilling and tragic. Newspapers also employed illustrations and engravings that depicted Mary in an almost ethereal light, often juxtaposed with grim images of the crime scene. These visual elements were powerful tools, adding depth to the written word and making the story more compelling.

Public reaction to these sensational headlines was immediate and intense. People gathered in public squares and meeting halls to discuss the latest developments and share their own theories. The media coverage prompted letters to the editor, filled with expressions of shock and demands for justice. Citizens from all walks of life felt a connection to Mary, seeing in her a reflection of their own daughters, sisters, and wives. This collective outrage created a sense of urgency that permeated the entire city, turning Mary's murder into a cause célèbre.

The relentless media attention also had a strong psychological effect on the public. Every day, New Yorkers were bombarded with new details, theories, and graphic descriptions of Mary's death. This constant exposure to sensationalized headlines stirred a mixture of fear and morbid curiosity. The media had tapped into the public's fascination with crime while simultaneously stoking their anxieties. People began to wonder if a killer was lurking in the city, waiting to strike again. The demand for justice intensified as readers developed an emotional attachment to Mary, seeing her as a symbol of the fragility of life in a rapidly urbanizing environment. The case became a shared trauma, turning private fears into a collective obsession.

Media narratives heavily influenced public opinion. Newspapers shaped the way people understood the case, often presenting theories and speculations as facts. This had a profound impact on the perception of suspects and the direction of the investigation. For instance, when a headline suggested that a "tall, dark-complexioned man" was seen with Mary on the day of her disappearance, public suspicion quickly turned towards this unidentified figure. The media's portrayal of suspects influenced not only public sentiment but also law enforcement's strategies.

The sensational coverage of Mary Rogers' murder did more than just inform; it manipulated. By focusing on the most lurid details and speculative theories, newspapers created a narrative that fueled public fascination and outrage. This, in turn, put immense pressure on the authorities to solve the case quickly. The investigation was often swayed by the latest media-driven theories, diverting resources and attention based on the whims of public opinion. This dynamic was not lost on the newspapers, which continued to publish stories that would keep the public engaged and their sales high.

In this environment, the truth often took a backseat to sensationalism. The media's portrayal of Mary and the suspects was rarely nuanced, focusing instead on elements that would sell papers. This lack of balance and integrity in reporting had long-term consequences, shaping the public's understanding of the case in ways that were often misleading. Yet, it also highlighted the power of the press to influence social and cultural dynamics. The case of Mary Rogers became more than just a murder investigation; it was a reflection of the times, illustrating the complex interplay between media, public opinion, and justice.

The legacy of these sensational headlines is still felt today. Modern true crime media, with its podcasts, television shows, and online platforms, often follows a similar playbook. The use of dramatic language and compelling visuals continues to draw audiences, shaping public perception and influencing the course of investigations. The story of Mary Rogers serves as a poignant reminder of the enduring power of sensationalism in media, a force that can both illuminate and obscure the truth.

The sensationalism of the penny press in the 19th century mirrors the challenges we face in the modern digital landscape. Today, social media and online news sites often prioritize engagement over accuracy, leading to the rapid spread of misinformation. Just as 19th-century readers were drawn to scandalous headlines, modern audiences are enticed by clickbait and sensational stories that often blur fact and fiction. Viral articles, manipulated images, and the speed at which news circulates make it even harder to discern truth from sensationalism. The parallels between the penny press and today's media demonstrate the enduring struggle between journalistic integrity and the public's insatiable appetite for dramatic stories.

The Media's Impact on the Investigation

The media's role in the Mary Rogers case was far from passive; it actively interfered with the investigation, often to its detriment. Journalists, driven by the need to get the scoop, frequently disrupted police work. Crime scenes were not sacrosanct; they were open fields for reporters eager to capture the minutiae of the tragedy. Their presence often contaminated crucial evidence, making it difficult for authorities to conduct a thorough investigation. Confidential information, once guarded by the police, found its way onto the front pages of newspapers, leaving the authorities scrambling to manage both public expectations and the integrity of their investigation.

The intense media scrutiny placed immense pressure on law enforcement to act swiftly. Public demands for quick results led to hasty actions that compromised the quality of the investigation. The pressure to identify and arrest suspects quickly often overshadowed the need for meticulous, evidence-based police work. This rush to judgment was not just a reflection of the media's influence but also of a public eager for closure in a case that had captured their collective imagination. The authorities found themselves in a precarious position, balancing the need for thoroughness with the public's clamor for swift justice. This dynamic often resulted in shortcuts and oversights that would haunt the investigation for years to come.

The media did not merely report on the investigation; it shaped it. Newspapers promoted specific theories and suspects, influencing both public opinion and police focus. One paper might endorse the idea of a jealous lover, while another pushes the theory of a gang-related crime. These media-driven theories often diverted the investigation, leading to wasted resources and missed opportunities. The police, under immense public pressure, were sometimes swayed by these narratives, prioritizing leads that were more sensational than substantive. This interplay between media and law enforcement created a feedback loop in which each influenced the other, often to the detriment of uncovering the truth.

The long-term effects of media involvement in the Mary Rogers case are still felt. The enduring public fascination with the case stems in large part from the media's sensational coverage. This fascination has kept the story alive in the public memory, making it a touchstone for discussions about media influence and investigative practices. The case has also had a lasting impact on investigative journalism. The coverage of Mary Rogers' murder set a precedent for how the media engages with high-profile crimes, blending fact and fiction in ways that captivate but also distort.

The legacy of this media involvement is a double-edged sword. On one hand, it highlights the power of the press to bring attention to important issues and keep them in the public eye. On the other hand, it underscores the potential for media to manipulate and mislead, shaping narratives that prioritize sensationalism over truth. This duality is a crucial aspect of understanding the Mary Rogers case and its place in the broader context of media influence on crime investigations.

Comparing Media Coverage: Then and Now

The media landscape during Mary Rogers' time was starkly different from what we experience today. In the 19th century, news traveled primarily through printed newspapers, which were the primary source of public information. The technology of the time limited how quickly and widely information could spread. Printing presses were either manual or steam-powered, and newspaper distribution was a labor-intensive process. Journalistic standards were still evolving, and ethics often took a backseat to sensationalism and sales. Today, digital technology allows news to spread instantaneously across the globe. Social media platforms, online news sites, and 24-hour news channels ensure that information is continuously available and updated in real-time. This rapid dissemination of news has transformed how people consume and interact with information.

Modern true crime coverage has leveraged these technological advancements to create a more immersive and engaging experience for audiences. Television shows, podcasts, and online platforms have become the new frontiers for storytelling in the true crime genre. Popular podcasts like "Serial" and TV shows like "Making a Murderer" have captivated millions, combining meticulous research with compelling narratives. These platforms offer a deeper dive into cases, often providing new insights and perspectives. Social media plays a crucial role in publicizing and discussing these cases, creating communities of amateur sleuths who analyze evidence, share theories, and engage in discussions. This level of public engagement was unimaginable in the 19th century, when the flow of information was unidirectional, from the newspapers to the readers.

Sensationalism continues to be a powerful force in modern media, much like it was during Mary Rogers' time. Viral news stories and clickbait headlines dominate the digital landscape, drawing readers in with promises of shocking revelations and dramatic twists. The quest for clicks and views often leads to the exaggeration or distortion of facts, influencing public perception in significant ways. This sensationalism can skew the understanding of a case, much as it did in the 19th century when newspapers sensationalized Mary's murder. The public's fascination with crime stories is fueled by this sensationalism, driving engagement and, in some cases, even affecting the course of investigations.

The internet has amplified the role of public engagement and amateur sleuthing. Online forums and social media platforms provide spaces for individuals to dissect cases, share information, and propose theories. This collective effort can sometimes unearth new evidence or bring fresh perspectives to old cases. However, it also carries the risk of spreading misinformation and drawing false conclusions. The democratization of information means that anyone with an internet connection can weigh in on a case, for better or worse. The balance between public interest and responsible journalism becomes even more critical in this context.

Reflecting on lessons from historical cases like Mary Rogers's can offer valuable insights for modern journalists and investigators. Ethical considerations in reporting on active investigations are paramount. The rush to publish sensational stories should not come at the expense of accuracy and integrity. Journalists must navigate the fine line between informing the public and respecting the privacy and dignity of those involved. Balancing public interest with responsible journalism is a challenge that requires constant vigilance and a commitment to ethical standards. The case of Mary Rogers serves as a poignant reminder of the impact that media can have on public perception and the course of justice.

Understanding these dynamics can help ensure that modern media coverage does not repeat the mistakes of the past. By focusing on accuracy, context, and ethical reporting, journalists can provide the public with the information they need without compromising the integrity of the investigation. In doing so, they can honor the legacy of cases like Mary Rogers' by contributing to a more informed and just society. The ongoing fascination with true crime, both in the 19th century and today, underscores the enduring human interest in the mysteries of life and death. The media's role in shaping these narratives continues to evolve, offering both opportunities and challenges in the pursuit of truth and justice.

CHAPTER 5

EDGAR ALLAN POE'S INVOLVEMENT

In the heart of 19th-century New York, amidst the cacophony of horse-drawn carriages and the hum of urban life, Edgar Allan Poe found himself drawn to the enigmatic case of Mary Rogers, not just as a writer but as someone personally affected by themes of loss and mystery. Known for his gothic tales and poetic musings, Poe was also a keen observer of human nature and a burgeoning detective writer. His fascination with Mary Rogers' murder was not merely literary; it was deeply personal and reflective of his own struggles and obsessions.

While Edgar Allan Poe became engrossed in the Mary Rogers case, his personal life was a battlefield. Financial instability was a constant shadow, despite his growing reputation as a writer. His job stability was anything but secure, as he moved from one editorial position to another, often clashing with publishers who failed to appreciate his exacting standards. His troubled personal relationships compounded these professional struggles. His marriage to Virginia Clemm, his first cousin, was both a source of solace and a source of strain. Virginia's frail health added to Poe's anxieties, as he feared losing yet another loved one to the relentless march of illness.

Poe's Fascination with the Case

Poe's initial interest in the Mary Rogers case was sparked by his dual role as a writer and editor in New York. At the time, he was working for the New York Evening Mirror, a position that placed him at the epicenter of the city's media frenzy. His role demanded a keen eye for stories that would captivate the public, and Mary Rogers' murder was precisely that: a sensational tale that gripped the city's imagination. Poe's known interest in real-life mysteries and his fascination with crime stories made the case irresistible. He saw in it not just a story to tell but a puzzle to solve, a chance to apply his analytical mind to a real-world enigma.

These personal challenges took a toll on Poe's mental state. The pressures of financial insecurity and the fear of losing Virginia exacerbated his existing melancholia and anxiety. His involvement in the Mary Rogers case, while intellectually stimulating, also mirrored his own fears and struggles. The themes of loss and vulnerability in the case resonated deeply with Poe, reflecting the turmoil in his own life. The act of writing *The Mystery of Marie Roget* became a double-edged sword; both a means of escape and a reminder of his inner demons. The case, with its unresolved nature and tragic beauty, echoed the uncertainties that plagued Poe's existence.

Poe approached the case with the meticulousness of a seasoned detective, exemplifying his influence on detective fiction. He visited the crime scene, scrutinizing every detail with the precision of his fictional detective, C. Auguste Dupin. Poe wasn't content with second-hand accounts; he sought firsthand information, interviewing locals and gathering their observations. His visits to Hoboken, where Mary's body was discovered, were not mere morbid curiosity but a genuine attempt to piece together the clues. Poe's correspondence and discussions with other intellectuals of the time further enriched his understanding, allowing him to formulate theories that went beyond the sensational headlines.

Poe's philosophical views were profoundly influenced by the Mary Rogers case. His fascination with death and the macabre found new dimensions as he pondered the nature of crime and human frailty. In his letters and essays, Poe often reflected on the inevitability of death and the arbitrary nature of fate. The case reinforced his belief in the fragile veneer of civilization, beneath which lurked chaos and violence. He saw in Mary Rogers' murder a microcosm of human existence; an interplay of beauty and brutality, innocence and corruption. These reflections, with their depth and complexity, seeped into his writing, giving his work a depth and complexity that transcended mere storytelling and left his readers intellectually stimulated, which is essential for engaging scholarly and literary audiences.

Poe's motivations for delving into the Mary Rogers case were multifaceted. On a professional level, Poe recognized the potential for literary inspiration and public attention. A well-crafted narrative about the case could elevate his standing as a writer and satisfy the public's craving for resolution. But there was also a deeply personal dimension to his obsession. Poe's own life was riddled with struggles: financial instability, the loss of loved ones, and a constant battle with his inner demons. His fascination with death and the macabre was not merely a literary device but a reflection of his own existential anxieties. The case of Mary Rogers, with its themes of beauty, violence, and mystery, resonated deeply with Poe's own fears and obsessions, creating an emotional connection that fueled his exploration.

The case also prompted Poe to explore the philosophical implications of crime. He questioned the moral underpinnings of society and the ease with which innocence could be shattered. In his writings, Poe delved into the psychological motivations behind criminal acts, seeking to understand the darkness that drove individuals to commit atrocities. His characters often grappled with existential dilemmas, mirroring his own struggles with meaning and morality. The Mary Rogers case became a lens through which Poe examined these weighty themes, enriching his literary oeuvre with philosophical insights.

Poe's public commentary on the case further demonstrated his engagement. He wrote several articles and letters that articulated his theories and observations. In the pages of the New York Evening Mirror, Poe's analysis of the case stood out for its depth and insight. He critiqued the police investigation, identified inconsistencies in witness testimony, and suggested alternative scenarios that had been overlooked. His writings were not just speculative; they were grounded in the evidence he had painstakingly gathered. Public reactions to his commentary were mixed; while some praised his analytical skills, others saw him as an outsider intruding into a tragic affair. This varied response underscores the complexity of Poe's influence and the challenges he faced in shaping public views on crime and investigation, highlighting the intricacies of his impact.

Poe's involvement with the Mary Rogers case left an indelible mark on his legacy as a writer. His meticulous approach to the investigation and his ability to weave factual elements into a compelling narrative set a new standard for detective fiction. Subsequent writers drew inspiration from Poe's work, adopting his techniques of deduction and analytical reasoning. Poe's influence extended beyond literature; his approach to crime and investigation shaped public discourse and laid the groundwork for modern true crime narratives. His blend of fact and fiction, grounded in philosophical inquiry, resonated with readers and scholars alike, cementing his place as a pioneering figure in the genre.

The case of Mary Rogers added a layer of humanity to Poe's narrative. His own struggles with financial difficulties and job instability mirrored the precariousness of Mary's life. His troubled relationships and personal losses echoed the themes of vulnerability and danger that surrounded her.

This personal connection to the case infused Poe's analysis with a sincerity and urgency that resonated with readers. It was not just a story for him; it was an exploration of themes that haunted his own life.

Poe's involvement in the Mary Rogers case left a lasting legacy on the genre of crime investigation. His meticulous approach and analytical mind set a standard for future detective stories. The blend of fact and fiction in his writings influenced the way real-life mysteries were perceived and investigated. He introduced key detective fiction tropes, such as retracing the crime scene and the poetic impact of a beautiful woman's death, elements that would become staples of the genre. Poe's work on the Mary Rogers case not only added to his literary acclaim but also shaped public views on crime and investigation, laying the groundwork for the true crime genre as we know it today. His legacy in crime investigation is a testament to his enduring influence, leaving the audience with a sense of his lasting impact on the genre.

The legacy of Edgar Allan Poe's involvement in the Mary Rogers case is a testament to his enduring influence. His ability to transform a real-life tragedy into a compelling narrative not only captivated his contemporaries but also left an indelible mark on the world of detective fiction. The case, through Poe's eyes, became more than just a mystery; it became a lens through which the complexities of human nature and societal dynamics were explored. As you delve into this chapter, you will uncover the layers of Poe's fascination, motivations, and the profound impact he had on the narrative of Mary Rogers. This impact continues to resonate in the annals of true crime and literary history.

Writing "The Mystery of Marie Roget"

Edgar Allan Poe's process for writing 'The Mystery of Marie Roget' was deeply rooted in his meticulous research and creative genius. He began by immersing himself in newspaper reports and public records related to Mary Rogers' case. These sources provided him with a wealth of information, from witness testimonies to police reports, which he used to construct a detailed narrative. Poe's creative process was methodical; he carefully sifted through the facts, identifying the most compelling elements to weave into his story. His narrative choices were deliberate, aiming to create a tale that was both engaging and thought-provoking. This attention to detail and commitment to authenticity set Poe's work apart and contributed to its lasting impact on the genre of detective fiction.

Poe's use of newspaper reports was particularly significant. He pored over articles from the New York Sun and other publications, extracting details that would add authenticity to his story. His research extended beyond the printed word; he engaged in discussions with contemporaries who were familiar with the case, seeking their insights and opinions. This collaborative approach helped him refine his theories and enrich his narrative. As he drafted "The Mystery of Marie Roget," Poe blended these real-life elements with his imaginative prowess, creating a story that felt both realistic and fantastical.

In adapting the real-life events of Mary Rogers' case into the fictional story of Marie Roget, Poe made several key changes to fit his narrative structure. He shifted the setting from New York to Paris, a choice that allowed him to explore the case within a different cultural context. This relocation also provided a layer of distance, enabling readers to engage with the story as a work of fiction while still recognizing its real-life parallels. The character of Marie Roget was a clear reflection of Mary Rogers, both young women known for their beauty and tragic fates. However, Poe introduced new characters and subplots to enhance the mystery and complexity of the story.

One of the most striking parallels between Mary Rogers and Marie Roget was their public personas. Both women were admired for their charm and beauty, and both met untimely deaths that captivated the public imagination. Yet, Poe's narrative diverged in key areas to create suspense and intrigue. He introduced false leads and red herrings, elements designed to keep readers guessing. These narrative techniques added depth to the story, making it more than just a straightforward retelling of a real-life event.

Poe's literary techniques in "The Mystery of Marie Roget" were masterful. He employed deduction and logical reasoning, hallmarks of his detective fiction, to unravel the mystery. His protagonist, C. Auguste Dupin, used meticulous observation and analytical skills to piece together the clues, much like Poe himself had done in his research. The use of red herrings and false leads added layers of complexity, drawing readers into a web of intrigue. These techniques not only created suspense but also showcased Poe's ability to blend fact and fiction seamlessly.

The public and critical reception of "The Mystery of Marie Roget" was mixed when it was published. Some readers and critics praised Poe for his innovative approach and his ability to transform a real-life tragedy into a compelling narrative. They admired his logical reasoning and skill in crafting a suspenseful plot. However, others criticized the story for its complexity and the liberties Poe took with the facts. Some felt that his fictionalization of the case detracted from the gravity of the real-life events. Despite these critiques, the story cemented Poe's reputation as a pioneering figure in detective fiction.

"The Mystery of Marie Roget" had a significant impact on Poe's career. It demonstrated his talent for blending real-life events with fiction, a skill that would influence future generations of writers. The story introduced key detective fiction tropes that are still used today, such as the methodical detective and the intricate plot. Poe's work on this story not only added to his literary acclaim but also shaped the way crime stories were told and understood. His ability to create a narrative that was both engaging and reflective of societal issues left an enduring legacy in literature and true crime.

Literary Analysis: Fact vs. Fiction

Edgar Allan Poe's "The Mystery of Marie Roget" stands as a fascinating intersection between reality and fiction. When dissecting the story's accuracy, it's clear Poe meticulously incorporated many real-life details from Mary Rogers' case. For instance, both Mary and her fictional counterpart, Marie Roget, were known for their beauty and worked in public-facing roles, making them minor celebrities in their communities. Poe mirrored the discovery of Mary's body in the Hudson River by setting Marie's death in the Seine, maintaining the eerie circumstances of her demise. Yet Poe also took creative liberties, changing the location to Paris and altering specific details to fit his narrative structure better. These changes allowed him to explore the case from a new angle, offering solutions and speculations that, while fictional, added layers of complexity to the real-life mystery.

The thematic elements in "The Mystery of Marie Roget" are rich and multifaceted. Poe delved deeply into themes of death, beauty, and mystery, portraying Marie as a tragic figure whose allure and public persona masked a vulnerable and ultimately doomed existence. This portrayal echoes the societal views of female beauty and victimhood, highlighting how public fascination often turns women into symbols rather than seeing them as individuals. Urban anonymity and crime also play significant roles in the narrative. Poe captured the chaotic, impersonal nature of city life, where individuals can easily become lost in the crowd, making crimes like Marie's murder both shocking and, paradoxically, expected in such a setting.

Literary devices are Poe's strong suit, and he employed them masterfully to blend fact with fiction. His use of foreshadowing and symbolism adds depth to the story. For example, the serene yet sinister setting of the Seine River symbolizes Marie's hidden turmoil and the dark forces at play. Poe's narrative voice and tone are meticulously crafted to maintain suspense and engage the reader's analytical mind. His tone vacillates between detached observation and emotional involvement, mirroring the reader's own journey through the labyrinth of clues and red herrings. This approach not only keeps the reader engaged but also invites them to participate in the detective work, much like Poe himself did while investigating Mary Rogers' case.

Reader perception of "The Mystery of Marie Roget" was as complex as the story itself. At the time, many were captivated by Poe's ability to weave a plausible narrative that felt grounded in reality. The blend of fact and fiction was so seamless that some readers believed Poe had insider knowledge about the case, lending the story an air of authenticity and authority. This plausibility influenced public understanding of the Mary Rogers case, with some adopting Poe's speculative solutions as plausible explanations. The story's influence extended beyond mere entertainment; it shaped public discourse around the case, blurring the lines between reality and fiction in a way that only Poe could master.

The legacy of "The Mystery of Marie Roget" in shaping perceptions of crime and investigation is undeniable. Poe's work set a precedent for future detective fiction, introducing elements that would become genre staples. His meticulous attention to detail, combined with his ability to craft a compelling narrative, paved the way for subsequent generations of writers and investigators. The story's lasting impact on public views of crime is a testament to Poe's genius, illustrating how the interplay of fact and fiction can create a narrative that resonates deeply with readers, leaving an indelible mark on the cultural and literary landscape.

Poe's Personal Struggles and Perspectives

While Edgar Allan Poe became engrossed in the Mary Rogers case, his personal life was fraught with difficulties. Financial instability was a constant shadow. Despite his growing reputation as a writer, Poe's income remained erratic, and his job stability was anything but secure. He moved from one editorial position to another, often clashing with publishers who failed to appreciate his exacting standards. His troubled personal relationships compounded these professional struggles. His marriage to Virginia Clemm, his first cousin, was both a source of solace and a source of strain. Virginia's frail health added to Poe's anxieties, as he feared losing yet another loved one to the relentless march of illness.

These personal challenges took a toll on Poe's mental state. The pressures of financial insecurity and the fear of losing Virginia exacerbated his existing melancholia and anxiety. His involvement in the Mary Rogers case, while intellectually stimulating, also mirrored his own fears and struggles. The themes of loss and vulnerability in the case resonated deeply with Poe, reflecting the turmoil in his own life. The act of writing "The Mystery of Marie Roget" became a double-edged sword; both a means of escape and a reminder of his inner demons. The case, with its unresolved nature and tragic beauty, echoed the uncertainties that plagued Poe's existence.

The Mary Rogers case profoundly influenced Poe's philosophical views. His fascination with death and the macabre found new dimensions as he pondered the nature of crime and human frailty. In his letters and essays, Poe often reflected on the inevitability of death and the arbitrary nature of fate. The case reinforced his belief in the fragile veneer of civilization, beneath which lurked chaos and violence. He saw in Mary Rogers' murder a microcosm of human existence; an interplay of beauty and brutality, innocence and corruption. These reflections seeped into his writing, giving his work a depth and complexity that transcended mere storytelling.

The case also prompted Poe to explore the philosophical implications of crime. He questioned the moral underpinnings of society and the ease with which innocence could be shattered. In his writings, Poe delved into the psychological motivations behind criminal acts, seeking to understand the darkness that drove individuals to commit atrocities. His characters often grappled with existential dilemmas, mirroring his own struggles with meaning and morality. The Mary Rogers case became a lens through which Poe examined these weighty themes, enriching his literary oeuvre with philosophical insights.

Poe's involvement with the Mary Rogers case had a lasting impact on his legacy as a writer. His meticulous approach to the investigation and his ability to weave factual elements into a compelling narrative set a new standard for detective fiction. Subsequent writers drew inspiration from Poe's work, adopting his techniques of deduction and analytical reasoning. Poe's influence extended beyond literature; his approach to crime and investigation shaped public discourse and laid the groundwork for modern true crime narratives. His blend of fact and fiction, grounded in philosophical inquiry, resonated with readers and scholars alike, cementing his place as a pioneering figure in the genre.

In examining Edgar Allan Poe's personal struggles and perspectives, one gains a deeper understanding of the man behind the stories. His engagement with the Mary Rogers case was not merely a literary endeavor but a reflection of his own existential quest. The themes he explored, death, beauty, and the nature of crime, were not abstract concepts but lived realities that informed his worldview. Poe's ability to transform personal anguish into literary brilliance is a testament to his genius, and his work on the Mary Rogers case remains a shining example of his enduring impact on literature and society.

Poe's involvement in the Mary Rogers case was a defining moment in his career. It showcased his analytical prowess, his philosophical depth, and his ability to transform real-life events into compelling narratives. The case became a canvas on which Poe painted his most profound fears and insights, enriching both his own legacy and the genre of detective fiction. As we transition to the next chapter, we'll delve into the limitations of forensic science in Mary's case and how these constraints shaped the investigation.

CHAPTER 6

THE INVESTIGATION METHODS OF THE 1840S

Crime Scene Investigation in the 1840s

Imagine stepping into a crime scene in the 1840s. The scene is chaotic, filled with onlookers and the murmurs of curious neighbors. The air is thick with a mix of curiosity and dread. Investigators of the time faced a daunting task, armed with little more than their instincts and rudimentary tools. Upon arriving at the scene, their first task was to secure the area, a challenge given the lack of formal procedures and the sheer number of people eager to catch a glimpse. Preventing contamination was nearly impossible. There were no barricades, no crime scene tape, just the voices of officers and the hope that bystanders would heed their calls to step back.

While investigating Mary Rogers' case, it's essential to humanize the individuals involved, moving beyond their roles as mere suspects or witnesses. For example, Daniel Payne, Mary's fiancé, is often reduced to the role of a tragic figure overwhelmed by guilt and alcohol. Yet, he was more than that. By exploring Payne's emotional complexity and the pressures he faced, we can better understand his motivations and responses. Similarly, John Anderson, who owned the tobacco shop where Mary worked, should be examined as more than just a business owner. Both men had personal relationships with Mary, and their psychological states were deeply affected by her death, providing more context to the broader narrative.

Initial observations were crucial. Investigators relied heavily on their eyes and ears, making mental notes before committing details to paper. Sketches were drawn hastily, often by hand, capturing the scene in broad strokes rather than precise detail. Notes were taken, though the quality varied depending on the officer's diligence and skill. The lack of standardized procedures meant that each investigator's approach could differ significantly, leading to inconsistencies that would hamper the investigation. Documentation was sparse, leaving gaps that modern forensic methods could have easily filled.

Daniel Payne's devastation over Mary's murder can be viewed within the context of 19th-century societal expectations. Men of that era were expected to be strong, rational, and protective, yet Payne's inability to save Mary from her tragic fate highlights a deep vulnerability. His eventual decline into alcoholism reflects the emotional toll that societal pressures placed on men to uphold stoicism in the face of personal loss. Likewise, the cultural norms of the time shaped how Mary's public persona as a beautiful woman working in a male-dominated space was perceived, ultimately influencing how the investigation and media coverage portrayed her death.

One of the primary challenges faced by investigators in the 1840s was the lack of standardized training and procedures. Recognizing their efforts can inspire appreciation for the advancements in forensic science and the importance of systematic training today.

Resources and technology were limited. Investigators had to make do with what they had: basic tools like magnifying glasses and rudimentary measuring devices. The concept of preserving a crime scene was still in its infancy, and the tools to do so were virtually nonexistent. There was no photography to capture the scene as it was found, no advanced chemical tests to detect substances. These resource constraints significantly hampered the ability to gather and analyze evidence accurately, highlighting the primitive state of forensic science in the 1840s. Investigators relied on their senses, intuition, and the hope that they could piece together the puzzle with the limited resources at their disposal.

Evidence collection was a rudimentary affair. Visible evidence, such as clothing and personal items, was carefully gathered, though the methods used were far from scientific. Items were often picked up by hand, wrapped in whatever material was available; sometimes cloth, other times paper; and stored in boxes or bags. The concept of preventing degradation was understood in theory, but it was challenging to implement in practice. Environmental factors, such as weather and temperature, could easily compromise the integrity of the evidence. The lack of proper storage facilities meant that crucial items were often left vulnerable to contamination and decay.

Witness testimony was a cornerstone of investigations in the 1840s. With limited physical evidence, the accounts of those who had seen or heard something became invaluable. Interview techniques were basic, often consisting of straightforward questioning without the benefit of modern psychological insights. Statements were recorded in notebooks, their accuracy dependent on the skill and honesty of both the witness and the interviewer. Assessing credibility was a challenge; there were no lie detectors, no methods to cross-check stories with forensic evidence. Investigators had to rely on their judgment, reading the body language and inconsistencies in the testimonies to gauge reliability.

The process of interviewing witnesses was fraught with difficulties. People's memories were fallible, influenced by their emotions and the passage of time. Some witnesses, eager to be helpful or gain attention, might embellish their accounts. Others, fearful of involvement, might hold back crucial details. Investigators had to navigate these complexities, sifting through the layers of truth and fabrication to find the facts. The reliability of a witness could make or break a case, adding immense pressure to get it right.

The case of Mary Rogers vividly illustrates the limitations of 19th-century forensic investigation. The bustling scene where her body was discovered was initially swarmed by onlookers, each step potentially destroying vital evidence. The officers' notes, while diligent, lacked the precision that modern documentation techniques, such as photography and detailed record-keeping, could provide. Witness statements varied, with some offering conflicting accounts that muddied the waters further. Each piece of evidence, from her disheveled clothing to the bruises on her body, was collected with care but without the benefit of advanced forensic tools that could have provided clearer answers. The reliance on witness testimony, while invaluable, left much to interpretation and the skill of the investigators.

The personal and psychological toll of Mary's death on those who knew her was profound. Daniel Payne's downward spiral and ultimate demise by suicide are stark reminders of how deeply traumatic events can shape the lives of those left behind. Payne's guilt and grief over his inability to protect Mary consumed him, and in examining his story, we can gain a deeper understanding of the emotional aftermath that violent crimes leave in their wake, both for those directly involved and the broader community.

The Role of Coroners and Medical Examiners

In the 1840s, the coroner was often the first official to arrive at a scene involving a sudden or unexplained death. Their primary duty was to conduct post-mortem examinations and determine the cause and manner of death. This role was critical in investigations like that of Mary Rogers, where understanding the nature of her injuries and the circumstances of her death could provide essential clues. The coroner's responsibilities extended beyond determining the cause of death; they also included identifying the deceased, notifying next of kin, and sometimes overseeing the collection of evidence.

The post-mortem examination process in the 19th century was rudimentary compared to today's standards. It began with a visual inspection of the body, where the coroner would look for any obvious signs of injury or struggle. This included noting bruises, cuts, and any other physical marks that could indicate foul play. The coroner would carefully document these findings, often with sketches or written descriptions, as photography was not yet a standard tool in forensic investigations.

Following the external examination, an internal examination would be conducted to identify any trauma or disease that might have contributed to the death. This involved opening the body and examining the organs for signs of injury, such as internal bleeding or damage to vital organs. The tools used for these examinations were basic: scalpels, saws, and rudimentary probes. The coroner had to rely heavily on their observational skills and medical knowledge, which varied greatly since many coroners lacked formal medical training.

The limitations of medical knowledge and technology at the time significantly affected the accuracy of the findings. Advanced diagnostic tools, such as microscopy and toxicology tests, were not available. Coroners had to make do with what they could see with the naked eye. This often led to incomplete or incorrect conclusions. The understanding of forensic pathology was in its infancy, and many causes of death could not be accurately determined without the advanced techniques we have today. For example, detecting poisons or subtle internal injuries was nearly impossible, leading to many cases being classified as "unknown causes."

In Mary Rogers' case, the coroner's role was pivotal yet constrained by these limitations. When her body was discovered, it was evident she had suffered a brutal assault. The external examination revealed signs of strangulation and multiple bruises, indicating a violent struggle. Her clothing was disheveled, and there were indications of a possible sexual assault. The coroner's report noted these injuries but could not definitively determine all the factors that led to her death. The lack of advanced forensic tools left many questions unanswered.

The coroner concluded that Mary had been strangled and beaten, but the exact sequence of events and the identity of her assailant remained elusive. The condition of her body, found days after her disappearance, complicated the examination. Decomposition had set in, further obscuring the details that might have provided more precise answers. The coroner's findings, while crucial, were limited by the tools and knowledge available at the time, leaving many aspects of the case shrouded in mystery.

In addition to Payne, John Anderson's involvement as Mary's employer sheds light on the complexities of social relationships and power dynamics in 19th-century America. Anderson, whose business thrived due to the allure Mary brought to his tobacco shop, likely faced his own internal conflicts after her death. Whether it was guilt, fear of public scrutiny, or a genuine sense of loss, understanding Anderson's role through a more empathetic lens provides a fuller picture of the tragedy, illustrating how economic and personal ties could intersect in such cases.

Both Payne and Anderson were men living under the weight of societal expectations that shaped their responses to Mary's death. The vulnerability Payne exhibited in the wake of his grief, descending into alcoholism and ultimately suicide, contrasts with Anderson's more subdued but complex emotional state. By considering the societal norms that influenced their actions, we see how both men were deeply affected by the intersection of gender dynamics and the cultural expectations of men in the 19th century.

In the 1840s, the coroner's office played a vital role in death investigations, though it was often hampered by the era's medical and technological constraints. Coroners had to rely on basic tools and their observational skills to determine the cause of death, usually facing challenges that modern forensic science has since overcome. The case of Mary Rogers illustrates both the importance and the limitations of the coroner's role in historical investigations. Her tragic fate, examined through the lens of

19th-century forensic practices, highlights the evolution of medical and investigative techniques.

Limitations of Forensic Science in Mary's Case

The investigation into Mary Rogers' murder in 1841 was plagued by the limitations of the era's forensic science. One of the most significant drawbacks was the inability to perform detailed toxicology tests. Detecting poisons or intoxicants was nearly impossible, as the advanced chemical analysis techniques we have today were non-existent. This limitation meant that any potential substances that could have incapacitated Mary or contributed to her death went undetected, leaving a crucial gap in the understanding of the crime.

Fingerprint analysis, a cornerstone of modern forensic science, was also unavailable. The concept of using fingerprints to identify suspects was still decades away from being developed. This absence left investigators without a reliable way to link individuals to the crime scene. DNA evidence, which revolutionized the field in the late 20th century, was an unimaginable tool for the 1840s. The lack of these advanced methods meant that investigators had to rely heavily on circumstantial evidence and witness testimony, both of which are prone to error and manipulation.

The emotional toll of Mary's death extended far beyond the forensic limitations of the era, as those closest to her became engulfed in the psychological aftermath. By exploring the mental states of individuals like Daniel Payne and John Anderson, we not only enhance our understanding of the case but also gain valuable insights into how trauma and grief can shape the narratives of criminal investigations. These portrayals help us appreciate the enduring complexity of human behavior in the face of tragedy, a factor that remains as relevant today as it was in the 1840s.

The implications of these limitations were profound. Without the ability to perform toxicology tests, the investigation could not determine if Mary had been drugged or poisoned before her death. This omission left a significant part of the puzzle unresolved. The absence of fingerprint analysis and DNA evidence made it nearly impossible to definitively place specific individuals at the crime scene. Investigators had to rely on witness testimony, which varied in reliability and detail. This reliance on circumstantial evidence often led to speculative theories rather than concrete conclusions.

Linking suspects to the crime scene proved to be a Herculean task. Without the tools to analyze blood, hair, or fibers, investigators could not establish a physical connection between Mary and her potential assailants. This gap forced them to focus on individuals' behaviors and movements, which were often based on hearsay and incomplete accounts. The difficulty in establishing a direct link to the crime scene led to many suspects being considered. Then it was dismissed on flimsy evidence, prolonging the investigation and complicating it further.

Comparing these limitations to modern forensic capabilities highlights the stark differences in investigative power. Today, DNA analysis and genetic profiling allow investigators to identify suspects with a high degree of accuracy, even from minute traces of biological material. Modern toxicology tests can detect a wide range of substances in a victim's system, providing insights into whether they were incapacitated or poisoned. These advancements have transformed the way crimes are investigated, offering tools that can give definitive answers rather than speculative theories.

In Mary Rogers' case, modern forensic methods could have made a significant difference. The potential analysis of blood or tissue samples could have revealed whether she had been drugged or poisoned. DNA evidence could have identified the individuals who were with her in her final hours, providing leads that were not available to the investigators of the time. The ability to reconstruct the crime scene using modern technology, such as 3D imaging and advanced chemical analysis, could have offered a clearer picture of her final moments and the events leading up to her death.

The limitations of forensic science in the 1840s not only hindered the investigation but also shaped the narrative of Mary Rogers' case. The absence of definitive evidence led to a reliance on circumstantial details and the testimonies of often unreliable witnesses. This reliance created an environment in which theories flourished but concrete answers remained elusive. The case became a reflection of the era's investigative challenges, highlighting the gaps that modern forensic science has since filled. Yet, the questions that remained unanswered due to these limitations continue to haunt the story of Mary Rogers, leaving it an enduring mystery that fascinates and perplexes even today.

In the context of Mary Rogers' tragic end, these limitations are a stark reminder of the challenges faced by investigators of the time. The absence of advanced forensic tools left many avenues unexplored, contributing to the enduring mystery of her death. Each piece of evidence, each witness statement, was a fragment of a larger puzzle that, without the benefit of modern science, could never be fully completed. The story of Mary Rogers is not just a tale of a life cut short; it is a testament to the evolution of forensic science and the relentless pursuit of truth in the face of overwhelming odds.

While forensic science has evolved considerably, it's crucial to acknowledge that human psychology remains a constant in criminal investigations. Both past and present cases demonstrate that understanding the mental and emotional states of those involved can be just as critical as the physical evidence. Forensic psychology, which has become a pivotal tool in modern-day criminal investigations, helps explain the motives, behaviors, and reactions of individuals in ways that forensic science alone cannot. In the case of Mary Rogers, understanding the psychological dimensions of figures like Payne and Anderson allows for a more complete interpretation of events, bridging the gap between historical context and modern analysis.

Comparing 19th Century and Modern Techniques

The evolution of investigative techniques from the 19th century to the present has been nothing short of revolutionary. In the early 20th century, the introduction of fingerprint analysis marked a significant leap forward. Before this, identifying suspects relied heavily on witness accounts and circumstantial evidence. Fingerprint analysis provided a reliable means of linking individuals to crime scenes, transforming investigative practices. Sir Francis Galton's work on fingerprint classification laid the groundwork, but its adoption by police forces worldwide truly changed the landscape of criminal investigations.

Forensic toxicology also saw substantial advancements. In the 1800s, detecting poisons was rudimentary at best. The development of more sophisticated chemical analysis techniques allowed for the detection of a wide range of substances, providing critical evidence in cases of suspected poisoning. The ability to analyze bodily fluids for toxins and drugs added a new layer of depth to forensic investigations, enabling more accurate determinations of the cause of death and uncovering foul play that might have otherwise gone undetected.

The advent of DNA profiling in the late 20th century was perhaps the most transformative breakthrough. This technique has revolutionized the field by enabling near-certain identification of individuals. DNA profiling has not only solved countless cases but has also exonerated those wrongfully accused. The impact on cold cases has been profound, with many long-unsolved crimes now being revisited and resolved thanks to this powerful tool. Advances in forensic pathology and medical imaging have further enhanced the accuracy of criminal investigations. Techniques like MRI and CT scans allow for non-invasive internal examinations, providing detailed insights into injuries and causes of death that were previously unattainable with traditional autopsies.

Modern investigators have a suite of advanced tools at their disposal that would have been unimaginable in the 1840s. Forensic databases, such as CODIS (Combined DNA Index System), enable the comparison of DNA samples from crime scenes with millions of profiles, drastically increasing the chances of finding matches. Digital evidence analysis has become crucial in the age of technology, allowing investigators to track communications, financial transactions, and other digital footprints that can provide vital clues. Forensic anthropology and odontology offer specialized techniques to analyze human remains and dental records, often identifying victims and providing critical information about the circumstances of their deaths.

The impact of these advancements on criminal investigations cannot be overstated. The accuracy and efficiency with which crimes can now be solved have dramatically improved. The ability to exonerate wrongfully accused individuals is a testament to the power of modern forensic science. Numerous cases of wrongful convictions have been overturned thanks to DNA evidence, highlighting the importance of these advancements in ensuring justice. The enhanced capability to solve complex, long-standing cases has brought closure to countless families and communities, providing answers that were previously out of reach.

In reflecting on these advancements, it is clear that the journey from the rudimentary techniques of the 19th century to the sophisticated methods of today has been driven by a relentless pursuit of accuracy and truth. Each breakthrough has built upon the last, creating a robust framework for modern forensic science. The ability to revisit cold cases and apply new techniques has breathed new life into investigations that once seemed hopeless. The story of Mary Rogers, viewed through the lens of modern forensic capabilities, underscores the profound impact these advancements have had on our understanding of criminal investigations.

As we conclude this chapter, consider the evolution of investigative techniques and their role in shaping the pursuit of justice. Advancements in forensic science have not only improved the accuracy and efficiency of investigations but also transformed our approach to solving crimes. In the next chapter, we will delve into the societal and cultural impact of Mary Rogers' case, exploring how her tragic fate resonated through the fabric of 19th-century America and beyond.

CHAPTER 7

KEY SUSPECTS AND THEORIES

July 28, 1841, was a day that would forever alter the course of Daniel Payne's life. The discovery of Mary Rogers' body in the Hudson River not only shattered his heart but also thrust him into the harsh spotlight of suspicion. As Mary's fiancé, Daniel was one of the closest people to her, and his actions and emotional state following her disappearance were scrutinized with an intensity that few could withstand. His story is one of love, despair, and the relentless pursuit of answers in a world that suddenly seemed devoid of them.

Daniel Payne: The Fiancé's Perspective

Daniel Payne, a cork cutter by trade, was a man of modest means but strong character. His profession, though humble, provided him with a stable income and a respected place within his community. Daniel boarded at the Rogers' house, where he met Mary. Their relationship blossomed quickly, marked by mutual affection and a shared vision of the future. Yet, like all relationships, theirs had its complexities. The pressures of societal expectations, particularly the rigid gender roles and the public scrutiny of Mary's role as the "Beautiful Cigar Girl," a term used to describe women who worked in cigar stores and were often objectified, occasionally led to tensions between them.

Despite these challenges, Daniel and Mary were deeply committed to each other. Their engagement was a promise of a life together, one that Daniel cherished and looked forward to with great anticipation. However, the idyllic vision of their future was shattered by Mary's sudden disappearance. Daniel's world turned upside down, and his actions in the days that followed reflected the depths of his despair. He joined the search efforts with a fervor that bordered on desperation, scouring the city and questioning anyone who might have seen Mary. His involvement was not just a duty; it was an expression of his love and an attempt to hold onto the hope that she would return unharmed.

When Mary's body was discovered, the community's collective mourning was palpable. Daniel, publicly distraught, his face a mask of sorrow, resonated with the community's shared grief. His visible grief aimed to evoke empathy, making the audience feel connected to the community's loss and Daniel's suffering.

The evidence against Daniel was circumstantial but compelling enough to warrant suspicion. Testimonies from those who interacted with him after Mary's disappearance painted a picture of a man on the edge. His account of the last time he saw Mary was consistent, but he struggled to fill in the gaps in his timeline convincingly. Some witnesses claimed that Daniel had been seen near the crime scene on the day of Mary's disappearance, though these sightings were never definitively proven. The most damning piece of evidence was his own admission of feeling an overwhelming sense of guilt, a statement that investigators interpreted as a possible confession, despite the lack of direct evidence linking him to the crime.

Daniel's behavior grew increasingly erratic in the weeks following Mary's death. He was often seen wandering the streets, lost in thought and visibly distressed. His involvement in the investigation became obsessive as he sought answers that seemed just out of reach. Friends and family members tried to support him, but their efforts were often met with resistance. Daniel's downward spiral culminated in his tragic suicide on October 7, 1841, a final act of despair that not only left more questions than answers but also significantly complicated the case.

However, not everyone believed Daniel was guilty. Many who knew him vouched for his character and his love for Mary. They described him as a gentle soul, incapable of the violence that had taken Mary's life. His close friends and family members provided statements that painted a different picture of his actions and emotional state. They spoke of his tireless efforts to find Mary, his genuine grief, and his unwavering commitment to uncovering the truth. These testimonies suggested that his erratic behavior was not an indication of guilt but rather a manifestation of his profound loss.

Community leaders, public intellectuals, and social activists played a crucial role in shaping the discourse that arose from the Mary Rogers case. Their collective action, driven by public demand for justice, led to early discussions of police reforms and the protection of vulnerable individuals. This highlights the power of community-driven change, inspiring hope for societal progress.

Alternative perspectives on Daniel's involvement explored the possibility of his innocence. Some argued that his inconsistencies were the result of trauma and grief, not deception. Recognizing his emotional turmoil encourages the audience to feel compassion and understand the human complexity behind his actions.

In the end, Daniel Payne's story is a tragic chapter in the mystery of Mary Rogers' murder. His love for Mary, his descent into despair, and his ultimate demise add layers of complexity to an already enigmatic case. While the evidence against him raised suspicions, the alternative perspectives provided by those who knew him best offer a more nuanced view of his character and actions. Daniel's fate, much like Mary's, remains a poignant reminder of the human cost of this mystery.

The sociopolitical implications of the Mary Rogers case continue to resonate in modern discussions about crime, gender, and the role of the media. Much like in today's true crime culture, the case highlighted how media sensationalism shapes public opinion and influences investigations. The scrutiny surrounding Mary's death, fueled by sensationalized media coverage, echoes contemporary conversations about the portrayal of women in the media, the handling of high-profile crimes, and the lasting impact of such cases on social reform.

The Mary Rogers case resonated far beyond the immediate tragedy, influencing political and social reforms aimed at urban safety and women's rights. The shocking nature of Mary's death, combined with the sensational media coverage, sparked public outrage and prompted calls for greater protection for women in urban environments. Her case catalyzed changes in policing practices and the establishment of early advocacy movements for women's safety, laying the groundwork for future reforms in both criminal justice and gender equality. The lasting impact of the Mary Rogers case on social reform is a testament to the event's significance.

John Anderson: The Employer's Angle

John Anderson was a man of ambition and shrewd business acumen. As the proprietor of John Anderson's Tobacco Emporium, he had carved out a significant niche in New York City's bustling commercial landscape. His shop, a popular haunt for locals and visitors alike, was known for its high-quality cigars and the charming presence of Mary Rogers. Anderson's career trajectory was marked by a series of calculated moves that elevated him from a modest background to a respected figure in the community. His reputation, however, was a double-edged sword. While many admired his business sense, others whispered about his ruthlessness and willingness to do whatever it took to succeed.

Mary Rogers' employment at Anderson's shop was more than just a job; it was a pivotal chapter in her life. Anderson recognized Mary's charm and used it to his advantage, positioning her as the 'Beautiful Cigar Girl' to attract customers. Their relationship, though professional, was complex. Anderson was both a mentor and a boss, guiding Mary in her role while also benefiting from the attention she drew to the shop. Despite their seemingly harmonious working relationship, the dynamics were not without tension. Some speculated that Anderson harbored personal feelings for Mary, feelings that may have been unreciprocated, leading to potential conflicts and jealousy that could have had implications for the case.

Theories about Anderson's involvement in Mary's murder stem from these underlying tensions. Some believed that a professional conflict could have escalated into something more sinister. Anderson's reliance on Mary for the shop's success might have created a volatile mix of dependence and resentment. Additionally, rumors suggested that Anderson's interest in Mary went beyond a professional capacity. If true, unrequited affection or jealousy could have provided a motive for a crime of passion. The possibility that Anderson saw Mary's increasing desire for independence as a threat to his business adds another layer of complexity.

The evidence against Anderson was circumstantial but intriguing. Coworkers and customers at the tobacco shop provided mixed accounts of his behavior. Some described him as a demanding employer who occasionally disagreed with Mary, while others noted his seemingly genuine concern for her well-being. Inconsistencies in Anderson's statements during the investigation raised eyebrows. At times, he appeared evasive, unable to provide a clear alibi for the crucial hours when Mary went missing. His initial reaction to her disappearance, characterized by a mix of panic and overzealous involvement, added to the suspicion.

Several coworkers reported instances in which Anderson's behavior towards Mary seemed overly familiar, blurring the lines between professional and personal interests. One particular incident involved a heated argument overheard by a regular customer, which fueled speculation about underlying tensions. These accounts, while not definitive, painted a picture of a relationship that was far from straightforward. The lack of concrete evidence, however, meant that these suspicions remained just that: suspicions.

In the face of these accusations, Anderson maintained his innocence with unwavering confidence. He made public statements expressing his sorrow over Mary's death and his commitment to finding the culprit. Anderson's interviews with the press were carefully crafted, portraying him as a concerned employer devastated by the loss of a valued employee. He offered a substantial reward for information leading to the capture of Mary's killer, a move that some saw as a genuine effort to seek justice. In contrast, others viewed it as a calculated attempt to deflect suspicion.

Supporters of Anderson provided testimonies vouching for his character and actions following Mary's disappearance. Longtime customers and business associates described him as a man of integrity, dedicated to his work and his employees. They pointed to his proactive role in the search efforts and his financial contributions as evidence of his innocence. Anderson's alibis, though initially questioned, were eventually supported by several credible witnesses who confirmed his whereabouts during the critical time frame.

John Anderson's involvement in Mary Rogers' life and subsequent murder investigation is a story filled with contradictions. His reputation as a successful businessman was both his shield and his Achilles' heel. The professional and personal dynamics between him and Mary added layers of complexity to an already intricate case. While the evidence against him was not definitive, the suspicions and rumors swirling around his name reflected the broader uncertainties and anxieties of a city grappling with a tragic mystery.

The Gang Theory: A Crime of Opportunity?

The theory that a local gang murdered Mary Rogers reflects the turbulent times of 1840s New York City, a period marked by rapid urbanization and growing social unrest. Gangs were an integral yet dark part of the city's underbelly, operating with a level of impunity that made them both feared and notorious. Among the most infamous were the Forty Thieves, the Bowery Boys, and the Dead Rabbits, each leaving a trail of violence and crime in their wake. These groups thrived in the chaotic environment of lower Manhattan, engaging in activities that ranged from petty theft to brutal assaults and even murder. Their presence instilled fear in the city's residents, and their exploits were frequently chronicled in the sensationalist press of the time.

Evidence supporting the gang theory emerged from various witness accounts and patterns observed in other crimes attributed to these groups. On the day Mary disappeared, several witnesses reported seeing men of rough demeanor loitering near the area where her body was later found. These men, described as intimidating and suspicious, matched the profiles of known gang members. Additionally, the brutal nature of Mary's death, strangulation accompanied by signs of a violent struggle, bore similarities to other crimes committed by gangs during that period. The discovery of her personal items scattered near Nick Moore's Roadhouse, a location known for its association with criminal activities, further fueled speculation about gang involvement.

Analyzing the plausibility of this theory requires a careful examination of the available evidence and historical context. On one hand, the presence of gang activity in the area and the violent manner of Mary's death lend credence to the idea that she could have fallen victim to a random act of gang violence. Gangs were known to target individuals for robbery or simply to assert their dominance, making Mary an unfortunate casualty in their ongoing reign of terror. The method of her murder, strangulation and a beating, was consistent with the brutal tactics employed by these groups, who often used excessive violence to instill fear and maintain control.

However, the gang theory also has weaknesses that cannot be overlooked. For one, gangs typically targeted individuals for tangible gains, such as money or valuables, yet there was no clear evidence that Mary was robbed. Additionally, while witness accounts placed suspicious individuals near the scene, these descriptions were vague and lacked the specificity needed to definitively link any particular gang to the crime. The chaotic, often unreliable nature of witness testimonies further complicates the matter, as memories may have been distorted by the emotional intensity of the situation and by the passage of time.

Law enforcement's response to the gang theory was a mix of targeted efforts and broader actions aimed at curbing gang activity in the city. Police made several attempts to infiltrate and dismantle local gangs, conducting raids on known hideouts and arresting key figures in an effort to gather information about Mary's murder. These efforts, however, were met with limited success. The secretive, tightly knit nature of these groups made it difficult for outsiders to penetrate their ranks, and the fear of retribution discouraged many potential informants from coming forward. Despite these challenges, the police remained vigilant, recognizing that gang-related violence posed a significant threat to the safety and stability of the city.

The public reaction to the gang theory was one of heightened fear and speculation. Newspapers fueled this anxiety with stories that painted a stark picture of a city under siege by ruthless criminals. Headlines screamed of gang-related atrocities, and the possibility that Mary Rogers had become the latest victim added a layer of urgency to the collective consciousness. Public meetings were held, and community leaders called for increased police presence and more stringent measures to combat gang violence. This atmosphere of fear and uncertainty permeated everyday life, affecting how residents navigated the city and interacted with one another.

In the end, the gang theory remains one of many plausible explanations for the tragic fate of Mary Rogers. It reflects the complexity of the social dynamics at play during a tumultuous period in New York City's history. While the evidence supporting this theory is compelling, it is not definitive, leaving room for continued debate and investigation. The enduring mystery of Mary's death is a testament to the challenges of solving crimes in an era where forensic science was still in its infancy, and the urban landscape was a labyrinth of hidden dangers.

Other Suspects and Unexplored Leads

As the investigation into Mary Rogers' murder unfolded, several lesser-known suspects emerged, each bringing their own shadowy complexities to the case. One such figure was a man named Charles Graham, a sailor who had been seen in the vicinity of the tobacco shop and was known to have harbored an infatuation with Mary. Graham's history of violent behavior and his proximity to Mary's workplace made him a person of interest. However, his alibi, corroborated by ship logs and fellow sailors' testimonies, ultimately led to his dismissal as a suspect. Another figure was Madame Restell, a notorious abortionist in New York City. Rumors circulated that Mary might have sought Restell's services, leading to a botched procedure and subsequent cover-up. Yet, an autopsy revealed that Mary was not pregnant, thus ruling out Restell as a viable suspect.

Beyond these individuals, there were several unexplored leads that investigators did not thoroughly pursue. One such lead came from a witness who claimed to have seen Mary with a well-dressed man near Castle Point just hours before she disappeared. This man, described as having a distinctive scar on his left cheek, was never identified or questioned. Another overlooked clue was a piece of fabric found near the crime scene that did not match Mary's clothing. Despite its potential significance, this evidence was not analyzed further, likely due to the limitations of forensic science at the time.

Neglecting these leads had a profound impact on the investigation's outcome. Each missed opportunity represented a potential breakthrough that could have brought clarity to the case. For instance, failing to identify the well-dressed man with the scar meant that a possibly crucial witness or suspect slipped through the cracks. The unexamined piece of fabric, had it been subjected to modern forensic techniques like fiber analysis, could have linked the crime scene to another location or individual. These oversights not only hindered the investigation but also shaped public and police perceptions of the case, often leading to speculative theories rather than concrete conclusions.

To consider alternative theories built on these unexplored leads is to open a new dimension of possibilities. One hypothetical scenario involves the well-dressed man being an influential figure who had reasons to remain in the shadows. Perhaps he was involved in illicit activities, using his social standing to avoid scrutiny. Another theory could involve the piece of fabric, suggesting a second crime scene or an accomplice who helped dispose of Mary's body. These alternative narratives, while speculative, provide fresh perspectives on the case and highlight the complexities of crime-solving in an era without the benefits of modern forensic science.

Introducing modern forensic methods into the context of Mary Rogers' case adds an educational layer for true crime enthusiasts. Today, DNA profiling can be used to analyze biological material found on the fabric, potentially identifying a suspect or at least narrowing down the possibilities. Advanced techniques like blood pattern analysis could have provided insights into the struggle that occurred, offering a clearer picture of Mary's final moments. The use of forensic genealogy might have identified distant relatives of the mysterious, well-dressed man, helping to trace his identity.

Comparing these modern methods to the rudimentary techniques available in the 1840s underscores the evolution of forensic science. Back then, investigators relied heavily on witness testimonies and basic physical evidence, often without the means to properly analyze or preserve it. The absence of standardized procedures meant that crucial evidence could be contaminated or overlooked entirely. Today's investigators have access to a plethora of tools and technologies that provide a more comprehensive understanding of crime scenes and suspects, reducing the margin for error and increasing the likelihood of solving cases.

Exploring the missed leads and alternative theories in Mary Rogers' case serves as a reminder of the limitations faced by 19th-century investigators. It also underscores the importance of thorough, methodical investigation practices, both then and now. The advancements in forensic science have revolutionized crime-solving, but the fundamental principles of careful evidence collection and analysis remain as crucial as ever. As we move forward, we will delve into the psychological profiles of key figures involved in Mary's life and death, offering more profound insights into their motivations and actions.

CHAPTER 8

PSYCHOLOGICAL PROFILES AND CHARACTER ANALYSIS

Mary Rogers was more than just a face in a bustling New York City tobacco shop; she was a complex individual whose life and tragic death left an indelible mark on those who knew her. To understand Mary, you must go beyond the headlines and public fascination, delving into the psychology of a young woman navigating the tumultuous landscape of 19th-century New York.

Women like Mary Rogers faced a daily battle to maintain their reputations while navigating a world where public and private expectations collided. Her role as the 'Beautiful Cigar Girl' placed her at the center of societal scrutiny, highlighting the delicate balance women had to uphold. On the one hand, she was admired for her beauty and charm, yet she was also subjected to the constant judgment of customers and society at large. Her every move was scrutinized, from how she presented herself in public to how she interacted with men. Public spaces, especially for women of working-class backgrounds, were fraught with the danger of losing respectability. The simple act of earning a wage outside the home was enough to raise eyebrows, but the nature of Mary's job, which involved engaging with male customers in a public setting, amplified the pressures she faced. The intense scrutiny of her personal and professional life left little room for error, forcing her always to present a polished and respectable image, no matter the internal toll it took on her mental health.

Mary Rogers' Psychological Portrait

Mary's personality was a testament to resilience, ambition, and social adeptness. Historical accounts and personal testimonies paint a picture of a young woman who, despite the challenges life threw her way, maintained a sense of grace and purpose. Her resilience, a quality that can inspire us all, was evident from an early age when she faced the loss of her father and the subsequent economic hardships. This formative experience likely nurtured a strength and determination that would define her later years. Mary's ambition was not just about personal success but about carving out a place for herself in a society that offered limited opportunities for women. Her role at John Anderson's tobacco shop was more than a job; it was a statement of her desire to assert her independence and make her mark.

Yet, beneath this veneer of resilience and ambition lay emotional vulnerabilities and fears. The pressure of being constantly in the public eye, combined with the societal expectations of the time, would have weighed heavily on her. Mary was known for her social skills, effortlessly engaging with customers and acquaintances alike. Her ability to navigate social situations with ease was both a strength and a coping mechanism, allowing her to mask any inner turmoil she might have felt. However, this public persona often concealed deeper emotional struggles. The constant scrutiny and the need to maintain a perfect image would have been exhausting, leaving little room for her to express her true feelings and fears. Recognizing these emotional struggles helps us understand her as more than just a victim of societal pressures, fostering empathy for her inner life.

The societal pressures of 19th-century New York were immense, especially for a woman in Mary's position. Women were expected to embody virtues of purity, modesty, and domesticity, and any deviation from these norms invited harsh judgment. Mary's role as the "Beautiful Cigar Girl" placed her under a spotlight that was both admiring and critical. Public scrutiny took a toll on her mental health, as she constantly balanced the expectations of her family, her employer, and society at large. Instances of public scrutiny were numerous, each one a reminder of the narrow path she had to tread. The disapproving glances, the whispered comments, and the media's fascination with her appearance all contributed to a relentless environment of pressure. Understanding these pressures can help us empathize with the challenges she faced.

Intersecting factors of gender, class, and race compounded the challenges faced by women like Mary. While Mary's beauty and role as the 'Beautiful Cigar Girl' elevated her to public fascination, her working-class background added a layer of vulnerability. Women of Mary's class were expected to work, but they were judged harshly for doing so, especially in public-facing roles. Additionally, while Mary herself was white, women of color faced even greater dangers in public spaces, where their bodies were often objectified or dismissed. For many women in the 19th century, navigating these intersections meant enduring daily harassment, limited employment opportunities, and the constant threat of public scandal. The rigid social hierarchies of the time dictated the roles women could occupy, and those who stepped outside these boundaries often faced harsh repercussions. Mary's experiences were not just a result of her gender but also her class and race, highlighting the intersectionality of societal pressures she faced.

Mary's coping strategies were a testament to her resilience in the face of societal pressures. She used her charm and social skills to navigate difficult situations, often using humor and grace to deflect criticism. However, this constant need to present a polished image was mentally draining, leading to moments of vulnerability and self-doubt. The emotional toll of societal pressures was profound, affecting her mental health in ways that were not always visible to those around her. Mary's coping strategies, while effective in many situations, also had their limitations, highlighting the complex interplay between her resilience and the societal pressures she faced.

Mary's relationships played a significant role in shaping her psychological state. Her bond with her mother, Phoebe, was particularly influential. Phoebe was both a source of strength and a reminder of the expectations placed on Mary. Their relationship, while loving, was also marked by the shared burden of economic survival and social propriety. Mary's friendships provided a semblance of normalcy and support, though her public persona often complicated them. Romantic relationships, particularly with her fiancé, Daniel Payne, added another layer of emotional complexity. The dynamics between Mary and Daniel were a mix of affection, tension, and societal pressure, each influencing her psychological well-being.

In the days leading up to her disappearance, Mary's psychological state showed signs of distress. Witnesses noted changes in her behavior, describing her as more introspective and quieter than usual. These subtle shifts hinted at underlying emotional turmoil. Possible triggers could have included the relentless public scrutiny, pressures from her relationships, or an impending sense of danger. Her final interactions, though seemingly ordinary, were tinged with an unspoken tension. Friends later recalled her appearing distracted, as if preoccupied with thoughts she couldn't share. These behavioral cues suggest a mind grappling with stress and fear, a young woman caught in the crosshairs of societal expectations and personal vulnerabilities.

Mary Rogers was a woman of remarkable strength and complexity. Her life, marked by moments of resilience and ambition, was also a story of emotional struggle and societal pressure. Understanding her psychological portrait provides a deeper insight into the tragic events that unfolded, shedding light on the human experience behind the historical mystery. Mary's story is a poignant reminder of the enduring impact of societal expectations on individual lives, a narrative that continues to resonate through the ages.

The gendered narratives surrounding Mary's case, focused on her beauty, her purity, and her perceived vulnerability, set a precedent for how women are often portrayed in true crime stories and media coverage. This case, like many others involving female victims, emphasized her attractiveness and victimhood rather than her individuality or personal agency. This emphasis on a woman's physical appearance and victim status has persisted into modern true crime narratives, where women are often depicted as passive figures whose stories revolve around their relationships to men or their roles as victims. Mary's story is a clear example of how these gendered frameworks shaped public opinion and continue to influence how we view women in both historical and contemporary true crime media.

Daniel Payne: Grief or Guilt?

Daniel Payne was a man marked by deep loyalty and emotional complexity. His dedication to Mary Rogers was evident to all who knew them, yet his personality was layered with traits that hinted at a more turbulent inner world. Known for his unwavering commitment, Daniel's loyalty was sometimes overshadowed by possessiveness. This possessiveness, while rooted in genuine affection, occasionally manifested as jealousy, creating friction in his relationship with Mary. His emotional volatility, a trait noted by friends and acquaintances, added to the complexity of his character. Daniel's history of mental health struggles, though not widely discussed at the time, played a significant role in shaping his responses to the events that unfolded. His emotional arc, from love and hope to grief and despair, provides a poignant lens through which to understand his behavior following Mary's disappearance.

In the days following Mary's disappearance, Daniel's reactions were a study in contrasts. Publicly, he was the image of a grieving fiancé, his sorrow palpable to those around him. He joined search efforts with a fervor that spoke to his desperation, often questioning potential witnesses and scouring the city for any sign of Mary. These public displays of grief were intense, his anguish visible in his every action. Yet, privately, Daniel's emotional state was even more volatile. Friends noted moments of profound despair, where he would retreat into silence or be overcome by sudden outbursts of tears. This duality, public sorrow and private torment, painted a picture of a man grappling with a loss that seemed too immense to bear.

However, Daniel's behavior also raised questions. Some observed actions and comments that, in retrospect, seemed suspicious. His intense grief sometimes bordered on the erratic, with moments that suggested more than just sorrow. For instance, his explanations for his whereabouts during critical times were inconsistent. These discrepancies, though perhaps understandable given his emotional state, fueled suspicions. Moreover, his suicide, which occurred near the spot where Mary's body was found, added another layer of complexity. Was it a final act of grief, or did it hint at a more profound sense of guilt?

Daniel's relationship with Mary was a blend of deep affection and underlying tension. Their bond was evident in their shared moments of love and commitment, yet it was not without its conflicts. Jealousy occasionally marred their interactions, and Daniel struggled to reconcile his possessiveness with his love for Mary. These moments of conflict, while not unusual in romantic relationships, were intensified by the public scrutiny they faced. Friends recounted episodes in which Daniel's jealousy flared, leading to arguments that, while resolved, left lingering traces of tension. Despite these conflicts, their relationship was also marked by genuine expressions of love and commitment. Daniel often spoke of their future together, his plans filled with hope and dreams of a life shared with Mary.

Considering the possibility of guilt requires a nuanced examination of Daniel's actions and psychological state. Several observers noted behavioral changes following Mary's disappearance. His emotional volatility increased with moments of irrational anger and profound sadness. These behavioral shifts, while possibly attributable to grief, also raised questions about his involvement in Mary's death. Inconsistencies in his statements to friends, family, and authorities further fueled these suspicions. Psychological analysis of his actions post-disappearance, including his suicide attempt, provides a complex picture. His final note, expressing remorse and a sense of a misspent life, could be interpreted in multiple ways. Was it an admission of guilt, a reflection of his grief, or a combination of both?

Understanding Daniel Payne's psychological profile offers insights into the emotional landscape that surrounded Mary Rogers' tragic end. His loyalty and love for Mary were genuine, yet his possessiveness and emotional volatility created a complex dynamic. His reactions to her disappearance and death, marked by intense grief and erratic behavior, raise questions that remain unanswered. The conflicts and expressions of love in their relationship, coupled with the psychological indicators of his potential involvement, paint a portrait of a man deeply affected by the events that unfolded. Daniel Payne's story, interwoven with Mary's, adds layers of emotional depth and complexity to the mystery, inviting you to consider the many facets of human emotion and behavior in the face of tragedy.

John Anderson: Victim or Villain?

John Anderson, the enterprising owner of the tobacco shop where Mary Rogers worked, was a man of ambition and undeniable charisma. His keen business sense had made his establishment a popular destination in New York City. People were drawn not only by the quality of his products but also by his charm. However, beneath this polished exterior, Anderson's personality was layered with complexities. His ambition was evident in his relentless drive to expand his business, often at the expense of personal relationships. Charisma helped him win over customers, but it also concealed a manipulative streak. Anderson knew how to use his charm to get what he wanted, a trait that served him well in business but raised questions about his personal integrity.

Anderson's relationship with Mary was multifaceted, blending professional interactions with undertones of personal involvement. As her employer, Anderson recognized Mary's ability to attract customers, a fact that did not go unnoticed by the patrons who frequented his shop. The power dynamic between them was palpable. Mary's role as the "Beautiful Cigar Girl" was both a blessing and a burden, elevating her status while subjecting her to Anderson's influence. Coworkers noted instances of favoritism, observing that Anderson gave Mary preferential treatment. This favoritism, while beneficial to Mary in some respects, also created tensions within the workplace. Colleagues whispered about the nature of their relationship, speculating whether it crossed professional boundaries.

Publicly, John Anderson maintained an image of a concerned and upstanding citizen. Following Mary's disappearance and the subsequent discovery of her body, Anderson was vocal in his expressions of sorrow and determination to find the culprit. His public statements were crafted to show solidarity with Mary's family and the community. He offered a substantial reward for information leading to the arrest of her killer, a move that garnered public praise. Yet, behind closed doors, Anderson's behavior told a different story. Those close to him reported a more calculated demeanor, one that was less about genuine concern and more about controlling the narrative. His private actions, marked by evasiveness and a lack of transparency, contrasted sharply with his public persona.

Evaluating the evidence of Anderson's involvement requires a careful analysis of both his alibi and his statements to the police. Anderson claimed he was at his shop during the critical hours of Mary's disappearance, a claim supported by some but contradicted by others. His alibi, while seemingly plausible, had gaps that investigators found troubling. These inconsistencies, coupled with his manipulative tendencies, cast doubt on his innocence. Psychological motives for harming Mary ranged from unreciprocated affection to a desire to silence any potential scandal that could damage his business. On the other hand, motives for protecting her included preserving his establishment's reputation and avoiding public backlash.

The discrepancies in Anderson's statements to the police further complicated the picture. Initial interviews showed him as cooperative, but as the investigation progressed, his responses became more guarded. This shift in behavior raised suspicions among investigators, who wondered if Anderson was hiding something. Witnesses from the shop provided mixed accounts: some described Anderson as genuinely distraught, while others noted a sense of detachment. These conflicting testimonies only added to the uncertainty surrounding his role in the case.

Psychologically, Anderson's actions can be seen through multiple lenses. His ambition and manipulativeness could have driven him to take drastic measures to protect his interests. Alternatively, his public displays of concern might reflect a genuine desire to see justice served, albeit clouded by his own self-preservation instincts. The complexities of his personality, combined with the power dynamics at play, make Anderson a figure of intrigue and suspicion. His involvement in Mary Rogers' life, both professional and potentially personal, places him at the heart of the mystery, a man whose true intentions remain as enigmatic as the case itself.

The Psychological Impact on Edgar Allan Poe

Edgar Allan Poe, a figure as enigmatic as the mysteries he wrote about, found himself deeply engrossed in the case of Mary Rogers. During this period, Poe's mental state was a complex tapestry woven from threads of depression, addiction, and financial instability. His life was marked by profound personal losses, including the death of his mother, his foster mother, and his young wife, Virginia Clemm, who was slowly succumbing to tuberculosis. These losses, compounded by his tumultuous career and frequent financial troubles, left Poe in a state of perpetual emotional turbulence. His alcohol addiction further exacerbated his mental fragility, creating a vicious cycle of despair and temporary relief.

Poe's fascination with the Mary Rogers case was not merely a professional interest; it was deeply personal. He saw in Mary's tragic end a reflection of his own obsessions with death and the macabre. This connection between his literary interests and personal struggles created a duality that was both therapeutic and damaging. On one hand, immersing himself in the case provided a distraction from his own sorrows, allowing him to channel his anxieties into his writing. On the other hand, the themes of violence and unresolved mystery in Mary's story mirrored his inner turmoil, often deepening his sense of despair. This intense involvement with the case became a way for Poe to grapple with his own demons, blurring the lines between his personal and professional worlds.

Poe's psychological state during this time is vividly reflected in his writing, particularly in "The Mystery of Marie Roget." The story, a thinly veiled retelling of Mary Rogers' case, is imbued with themes of death, loss, and unresolved mystery. Through his protagonist, C. Auguste Dupin, Poe explores the intricacies of human nature and the dark recesses of the human mind. The narrative is laden with literary devices that express Poe's emotional and psychological struggles. His use of detailed descriptions, logical deductions, and red herrings mirrors his own fragmented thoughts and the chaos of his life. The story's unresolved nature, with its lingering questions and ambiguous conclusions, parallels Poe's own sense of uncertainty and his quest for meaning in a world filled with loss and suffering.

The long-term impact of Poe's involvement with the Mary Rogers case on his life and career is profound. This period of intense focus on the case influenced his subsequent literary works, infusing them with a more profound sense of psychological complexity and existential dread. Themes of premature death, the mystery of the unknown, and the fragility of life became recurring motifs in his later stories and poems. Works like "The Tell-Tale Heart" and "Annabel Lee" echo the emotional and thematic elements he explored in "The Mystery of Marie Roget." These stories, while fictional, are imbued with the same sense of unresolved mystery and psychological depth that characterized his retelling of Mary Rogers' story.

Poe's reputation and public perception as a writer and intellectual were also shaped by his involvement with the case. His meticulous approach to the investigation, combined with his literary prowess, cemented his status as a pioneering figure in detective fiction. However, his personal struggles and erratic behavior often overshadowed his professional achievements, creating a complex legacy. Poe's life, marked by brilliance and tragedy, became intertwined with his literary creations, each influencing the other in a perpetual dance of art and reality.

As we close this chapter, reflecting on the psychological impact of the Mary Rogers case on Edgar Allan Poe, it's clear that the lines between investigator, writer, and troubled soul were often blurred. His literary contributions, shaped by his personal demons and professional pursuits, continue to resonate with readers and scholars alike. The next chapter will delve into the broader societal and cultural implications of Mary Rogers' murder, examining how this case influenced public perceptions and policies in 19th-century America.

CHAPTER 9

SOCIAL AND POLITICAL MANIPULATIONS

Mary Rogers' murder was not just a crime; it became a spectacle that was interwoven with the political and social fabric of 1840s New York. The city, teeming with life and change, was fertile ground for political maneuvering and public manipulation. As you delve into this chapter, imagine the bustling streets of a city on the brink of modernity, where every corner holds a story, and every story has the potential to sway the masses.

Political Climate and Public Opinion

In the early 1840s, New York City was a microcosm of the larger political tensions gripping the United States. The city was a battleground between the Democratic and Whig parties, each vying for control amid rapid urbanization and shifting demographics. The Democrats, championing the cause of the common man, often found themselves at odds with the Whigs, who represented business interests and the burgeoning middle class. Prominent figures like Martin Van Buren and William Henry Seward dominated the political landscape, their influence felt in every corner of the city.

The political environment was charged with issues that deeply resonated with the public, creating an atmosphere of urgency. Immigration was a hot-button topic, as waves of newcomers from Europe altered the city's social fabric. Urbanization brought both opportunity and chaos, with the city's infrastructure struggling to keep pace with its growing population. Crime and public safety became central concerns as traditional methods of maintaining order proved inadequate in the face of rising violence and disorder. The urgency of these issues was palpable, shaping the city's social and political landscape.

Mary Rogers' murder unfolded against a backdrop of political and social upheaval. The fear of escalating crime rates in a rapidly expanding city was palpable. Newspapers like the New York Sun and the New York Herald, with their sensational headlines, amplified this fear, feeding the public's anxiety. The gruesome details of Mary's murder, sensationalized by the media, became a focal point in discussions about urban safety, with many calling for improved law enforcement and public safety measures. The public demand for action was not just about solving Mary's case; it was a cry for order in a city that often seemed on the brink of chaos.

Politicians, always attuned to the pulse of public opinion, seized upon Mary Rogers' murder to further their own agendas. They crafted speeches and public statements to address the growing fear and outrage. Political figures, including city officials and law enforcement leaders, used the case to highlight their commitment to public safety and crime prevention. This led to specific legislative actions and policy proposals, such as increased funding for law enforcement, the establishment of a professional police force, and tougher penalties for criminals. Each of these measures was aimed at reassuring a jittery populace. The case became a rallying point for political opportunism, with every candidate eager to show that they could restore order and safety to the city.

The influence of Mary Rogers' murder extended into political campaigns and elections, demonstrating the power of public opinion. Candidates from both major parties used the case as a talking point in debates and rallies. Promises of increased funding for law enforcement, the establishment of a professional police force, and stricter penalties for criminals became staples of campaign platforms. The imagery of Mary Rogers, the innocent victim of a brutal crime, was invoked repeatedly to underscore the urgency of these promises. Voters, moved by the tragedy and the fear it engendered, responded to these messages, shaping the political landscape in profound ways. The power of the masses was evident in the shaping of these campaigns.

Reflecting on the political climate of the time, it's clear that Mary Rogers' case was more than just a murder mystery; it was a catalyst for political and social change. Politicians channeled the fear and outrage it generated into concrete actions and policies. The rhetoric surrounding the case highlighted the deep-seated anxieties of a city in transition, where the threat of disorder shadowed the promise of progress. As you navigate the complexities of this period, consider how the murder of one young woman became a symbol of the broader struggles and aspirations of a city poised on the edge of modernity.

Social Reformers and Moral Agendas

In the 1840s, New York City was a boiling pot of social reform, with courageous leaders and organizations emerging. Movements like temperance, anti-prostitution, and women's rights were gaining momentum. Figures like Dorothea Dix pushed for better treatment of the mentally ill, while temperance societies aimed to curb alcohol abuse. The Anti-Slavery Society, though primarily focused on ending slavery, also intersected with other social issues. They used rallies, pamphlets, and public speeches to spread their messages, reaching a wide audience eager for change. Mary Rogers' murder became a catalyst for these reformers, highlighting the urgent need for societal change and mobilizing the public for action.

Mary Rogers' murder became a moral touchstone for these reformers. They framed her death as a symptom of the broader societal ills plaguing urban areas. The dangers women faced in cities like New York were highlighted, with Mary's case serving as a grim example. Reformers argued that the city's rapid growth had outpaced its moral and social safeguards. They called for comprehensive reforms to protect vulnerable populations, focusing on improving public safety and ethical conduct. The murder was portrayed as a stark warning that without reform, more tragedies would follow. Mary's murder, therefore, played a significant role in galvanizing these social reform movements, providing a stark example of the urgent need for change.

Women's rights activists seized upon Mary Rogers' case to advocate for greater protections and rights for women. Leaders like Elizabeth Cady Stanton and Lucretia Mott used the case to spotlight the precarious position of women in society. Their writings and speeches emphasized the need for legal and social reforms to ensure women's safety. Public events and rallies were organized, drawing attention to gender-based violence and the urgent need for change. These gatherings were not just about mourning Mary; they were about mobilizing for a future in which such tragedies would become less likely.

Specific campaigns emerged in response to Mary's murder, focusing on issues like prostitution and women's employment conditions. Anti-prostitution activists linked her death to the dangers of the sex trade, arguing that women in such precarious positions were more vulnerable to violence. They pushed for stricter laws and better enforcement to curb the industry. Efforts to improve women's employment conditions also gained traction. Reformers argued that better job opportunities and safer working environments could prevent women from falling into dangerous situations. Mary's role as a public-facing employee became a focal point, illustrating the need for workplace reforms that prioritized safety and dignity.

Social reformers were adept at using Mary Rogers' murder to further their moral agendas. They framed the case to highlight societal failures and call for immediate action. Their arguments resonated with a public already anxious about urban crime and moral decay. By linking Mary's death to broader social issues, they were able to galvanize support for their causes. This strategic framing turned a tragic event into a catalyst for social change, showing how powerful narratives could drive reform.

Women's rights activists were particularly vocal in using Mary's case to push for legal and social changes. They argued that the conditions leading to her murder were not isolated incidents but part of a systemic issue. Legal protections, better employment opportunities, and societal respect for women's autonomy were seen as essential steps to prevent future tragedies. Their advocacy went beyond Mary's case, drawing attention to the everyday struggles and dangers women faced. Public rallies and writings by these activists created a groundswell of support, bringing women's rights issues to the forefront of public discourse.

Anti-prostitution campaigns gained renewed vigor in the wake of Mary Rogers' murder. Activists argued that the sex trade exposed women to severe risks, making them easy targets for violence. They called for stricter regulations and more robust enforcement to protect women from exploitation and harm. These campaigns were not just about morality; they were about safety and dignity. By framing the issue in terms of Mary's tragic fate, activists made a compelling case for urgent reform. The public response was significant, with many supporting the call for a cleaner, safer city where women could live and work without fear.

Efforts to improve women's employment conditions also gained momentum. Reformers highlighted the need for safer workplaces and better job opportunities for women. They argued that economic independence and secure working environments were crucial for protecting women from exploitation and violence. Mary's role at John Anderson's tobacco shop became a symbol of the precarious positions many women occupied. Campaigns focused on ensuring that women could work without facing undue risks, pushing for legislative changes and societal shifts to support this goal. These efforts were part of a broader movement to create a more equitable and just society for all.

The Case in Public Debates and Discussions

Mary Rogers' murder became a lightning rod for public discourse, igniting conversations across various forums, from newspapers to town hall meetings and social gatherings. Newspapers, the lifeblood of public opinion in the 1840s, were filled with editorials and opinion pieces dissecting every aspect of the case. The New York Sun and New York Herald led the charge, each offering its own interpretation and sensational spin. Town hall meetings became arenas for heated debates, with transcriptions revealing the raw emotions and varied opinions of the attendees. Social gatherings, too, buzzed with speculation, each conversation adding another layer to the already complex narrative.

The effectiveness of law enforcement was a recurring theme in these debates. Many questioned whether the existing police force, with its limited resources and outdated methods, was capable of solving such a high-profile case. Critics argued that the mishandling of the crime scene and the inconsistent statements from witnesses pointed to a deeper issue within the justice system. Discussions often turned to the need for a professional police force, echoing sentiments that had been growing louder since the rise in crime during the 1830s. The public's frustration was palpable, fueling demands for reform and more competent investigative practices.

The media's role in sensationalizing crime also dominated public discussions. While newspapers were instrumental in keeping Mary's case in the public eye, their tendency to blur the lines between fact and fiction drew criticism. Many felt that the sensational headlines and speculative stories not only muddied the investigation but also manipulated public sentiment. The debate extended to the ethical responsibilities of journalists, with some arguing that the media's primary role should be to inform rather than to entertain. The press's influence was undeniable, shaping both the investigation and the public's perception of Mary and her tragic fate.

Influential voices emerged from various sectors, each adding depth and nuance to the public discourse. Prominent journalists like James Gordon Bennett of the New York Herald used their platforms to sway opinion, often blending hard facts with evocative storytelling. Politicians seized the opportunity to align themselves with public sentiment, delivering speeches that promised swift justice and increased safety measures. Social activists, particularly those involved in women's rights and anti-crime movements, used the case to highlight broader societal issues and advocate for reforms to protect vulnerable populations.

Public intellectuals and community leaders also played significant roles in shaping the conversation. Figures like Horace Greeley, editor of the New York Tribune, offered thoughtful critiques of the socio-political landscape, urging readers to consider the more profound implications of Mary's murder. Community leaders organized forums and discussions, providing spaces where citizens could voice their concerns and ideas. These influential voices helped frame the narrative, guiding public opinion and keeping the issue at the forefront of societal debates.

The broader social implications of Mary Rogers' case were far-reaching. The intense public interest and subsequent debates influenced policy and social reform efforts, leading to concrete changes in how urban safety was approached. The case underscored the need for a more structured, professional police force, which contributed to the eventual establishment of the NYPD in 1845. It also highlighted the limitations of the existing justice system, prompting calls for judicial and procedural reforms. The public's demand for accountability and effectiveness in law enforcement found its way into legislative action, shaping policies aimed at creating a safer urban environment.

One of the most glaring examples of 19th-century forensic limitations was the inability to properly preserve crime scenes. In Mary's case, onlookers and curious neighbors freely walked through the area where her body was discovered, likely trampling over vital evidence. The lack of protocols for handling potential witnesses also contributed to confusion, with contradictory accounts of events muddying the investigation. Moreover, the absence of chemical tests and forensic tools, such as fingerprinting or blood analysis, severely limited the investigators' ability to connect Mary's assailant to the crime. Investigators were left to rely on rudimentary methods, such as noting visible bruises and making rough sketches of the crime scene, far from the detailed procedures that modern investigators take for granted.

The long-term changes in public attitudes toward crime and victimhood were significant. Mary's case brought to light the vulnerabilities faced by women in urban settings, sparking discussions about gender and safety that resonated far beyond her time. The public's perception of crime evolved, with a growing awareness of the complexities and systemic issues that contributed to such tragedies. These shifts in attitude were reflected in the increased support for social reforms, from better working conditions for women to more robust public safety measures. The case of Mary Rogers became a lens through which society examined its own moral and structural shortcomings, leading to a more conscientious and proactive approach to addressing urban crime and social justice.

The Mary Rogers case became a critical turning point in the public's demand for a more structured law enforcement system. The mishandling of her investigation highlighted the need for a professional police force capable of dealing with the complexities of crime in a rapidly growing urban environment. This public outcry for justice contributed to the eventual establishment of the New York Police Department in 1845, just a few years after Mary's death. The case also emphasized the importance of developing modern forensic techniques, underscoring the need for more scientific approaches to criminal investigations, such as proper evidence collection and the introduction of forensic pathology.

While forensic science has evolved tremendously since the 1840s, modern investigators still face challenges that echo those encountered in Mary Rogers' case. Today, the application of forensic techniques, such as DNA profiling and digital forensics, is not without controversy. Ethical considerations arise around privacy rights, the potential for forensic errors, and the misuse of forensic data in courtrooms. Just as in the 19th century, where incomplete methods often led to missed leads or wrongful accusations, modern forensic practices must grapple with ensuring accuracy, transparency, and fairness in a justice system that relies heavily on scientific evidence. Balancing the power of forensic science with ethical safeguards remains as crucial today as it was when Mary's case unfolded.

Manipulation of Public Sentiment

The media's role in the Mary Rogers case was far from impartial. Newspapers wielded their power to shape public sentiment, using strategies that blurred the line between news and sensationalism. Headlines screamed with drama, each one crafted to capture and hold the reader's attention. "The Beautiful Cigar Girl Found Dead!" and "Murder Most Foul: The Mystery of Mary Rogers" were more than just news; they were narratives designed to provoke an emotional response. Journalists often published speculative theories and unverified information, feeding the public's insatiable appetite for scandal and intrigue. These stories didn't just inform; they entertained, turning a tragic event into a gripping saga.

Public figures, too, were adept at manipulating sentiment to serve their own ends. Politicians, social reformers, and even local celebrities saw an opportunity in Mary's death to further their agendas. Public speeches and statements were carefully crafted to sway opinion, each word chosen to evoke sympathy, outrage, or a call to action. These figures strategically used Mary's image and story in their campaigns, aligning themselves with the public's desire for justice and safety. By portraying themselves as champions of the innocent, they garnered support and legitimacy, often at the expense of nuanced understanding.

The manipulation of public sentiment had a profound impact on the investigation. Law enforcement found themselves under immense pressure to deliver quick results, a demand that often led to hasty, ill-considered actions. Resources and attention were diverted from critical leads as police chased down every sensational theory that emerged in the press. The focus on high-profile suspects and dramatic narratives overshadowed methodical investigative work. This environment of urgency and spectacle hindered the pursuit of truth, creating a chaotic backdrop against which justice was hard to achieve.

Specific instances illustrate how public sentiment was manipulated in Mary Rogers' case. Rumors and misinformation spread like wildfire, each new piece of unverified information adding to the confusion. One notable example was the theory that Mary had been the victim of a botched abortion. This notion, though lacking substantial evidence, took hold in the public imagination, influenced by sensational newspaper articles and the era's moral anxieties. The focus on this theory drew attention away from other potential leads and suspects, skewing the investigation.

Campaigns leveraging the case for broader social or political goals were common. Social reformers used Mary's story to highlight the dangers faced by women in urban areas and to call for moral and social reforms. These campaigns, while aiming to address legitimate issues, often simplified Mary's life and death to fit their narratives. Politicians, eager to appear proactive, proposed new laws and public safety measures, each one framed as a response to the public outcry over Mary's murder. These actions, while sometimes beneficial, were also tinged with opportunism, driven by the need to appease a restless electorate.

The manipulation of public sentiment in the Mary Rogers case is a testament to the power of the media and public figures to shape the narrative. It shows how easily truth can be obscured by the demands of sensationalism and the agendas of those in power. This interplay among media, public opinion, and political maneuvering created a complex web that shaped the investigation's direction and effectiveness. As you reflect on these dynamics, consider how they resonate with modern instances of media influence and public sentiment, drawing parallels that highlight the enduring nature of these issues.

The case of Mary Rogers serves as a poignant example of how public sentiment can be both a tool and a weapon. It underscores the need for careful, ethical journalism and the importance of critical thinking in the face of sensational narratives. The next chapter will delve into the forensic limitations of the 1840s, exploring how these constraints shaped the investigation and the pursuit of justice in a rapidly evolving city.

CHAPTER 10

THE GENDER DYNAMICS OF THE CASE

In a world where societal norms cast long shadows, Mary Rogers' life and death were deeply influenced by Victorian era expectations. Highlighting how these pressures, like a heavy weight, shaped her world and fate helps readers understand the societal context that defined her story.

The Victorian Ideal of Womanhood

The Victorian era, spanning from the early 19th century to the turn of the 20th century, held a particularly rigid view of womanhood. Women were expected to embody purity, domesticity, and submissiveness. These qualities were not merely encouraged; they were demanded by a society that saw women as the moral and spiritual guardians of the home. The ideal woman was often referred to as the "Angel in the House," a phrase that epitomized the era's expectations. This perfect woman was expected to be selflessly devoted to her family, nurturing her children, and supporting her husband. Her virtue was her most prized attribute, and any deviation from this ideal was met with severe social censure.

In public and private life, modesty and decorum were paramount, and women were expected to dress modestly, speak softly, and act with unwavering propriety. Mary Rogers' role as a cigar saleswoman placed her at odds with these norms, illustrating the societal conflict she navigated.

Education and employment opportunities for women were starkly limited during the Victorian era. Educational institutions for girls focused primarily on teaching domestic skills and moral instruction. Subjects like cooking, sewing, and etiquette were emphasized over academic pursuits. The idea was to prepare women for their roles as wives and mothers rather than for any professional or intellectual endeavors. Employment opportunities were similarly constrained. Acceptable professions for women included teaching, domestic service, and occasionally nursing. These roles were seen as extensions of their domestic duties and were deemed appropriate because they aligned with the nurturing qualities expected of women.

These constraints significantly impacted women's autonomy and agency. Legal limitations were pervasive; women had few rights regarding property and voting. Married women, in particular, faced severe restrictions, as their legal identities were often subsumed under those of their husbands. This lack of legal autonomy meant that women had little control over their own lives and were largely dependent on male relatives for support and protection. Social stigma further reinforced these limitations. Women who defied traditional roles, whether by seeking higher education, engaging in unconventional employment, or displaying too much independence, were often ostracized and labeled as unfeminine or immoral.

The broader historical and cultural context of the 19th century played a significant role in shaping these gender norms. Religious and cultural beliefs, particularly the rise of evangelical Christianity with its emphasis on piety and morality, heavily influenced the construction of gender roles. These beliefs reinforced the idea of women as the spiritual backbone of the family. Cultural narratives in literature, art, and popular media further propagated these ideals, creating a pervasive and almost inescapable framework for women to navigate.

Comparatively, gender norms in other parts of the world during this period varied but often reflected similar patriarchal structures. In Europe, particularly in Britain and France, the ideals of domesticity and female virtue were equally strong. In contrast, some indigenous cultures in the Americas and Africa had different conceptions of gender roles, often allowing for more fluidity and autonomy for women. However, the spread of Western colonialism and its accompanying cultural imperialism usually imposed Victorian ideals on these societies, leading to a global reinforcement of restrictive gender norms.

Understanding the Societal expectations of women in the 19th century is crucial to understanding the world Mary Rogers inhabited. It underscores the immense pressure women faced to conform to these expectations, a weight that could be suffocating, and the severe consequences of deviating from them. Mary's work as a public figure in a male-dominated space not only challenged these ideals but also exposed her to heightened scrutiny and danger. Her life and untimely death highlight the complex interplay between societal expectations and individual agency, shedding light on the broader gender dynamics of the time.

Mary Rogers as a Symbol of Gender Issues

Mary Rogers' life and death serve as a poignant case study for understanding broader gender issues in the 19th century. As a working woman in a public-facing job, Mary defied the era's stringent expectations. Her role at John Anderson's tobacco shop was not just a job but a statement. In an age where women were expected to remain within the domestic sphere, Mary stood behind a counter, engaging with a predominantly male clientele. This visibility made her a subject of both admiration and scrutiny. Her beauty and social status added layers of complexity, transforming her into a public figure whose every move was watched and judged. This constant scrutiny undoubtedly had a profound impact on her personal life, blurring the lines between her public and private personas.

The artistic and literary representations of Mary Rogers' life and death have played a crucial role in shaping the public's perception of her. Authors like Edgar Allan Poe immortalized her story in works such as *The Mystery of Marie Roget*, intertwining fact with fiction in a way that captivated readers. These creative retellings often emphasized the tragic beauty of Mary's life, further entrenching her as an emblem of the era's moral anxieties. Over time, the line between Mary as an individual and Mary as a symbol of purity and vulnerability blurred, giving rise to a lasting cultural legacy. Visual art, too, contributed to this mythologizing, with illustrations of 'The Beautiful Cigar Girl' reinforcing her status as a tragic figure destined to suffer for her transgressions.

The public's fascination with Mary Rogers was a double-edged sword. While her charm and elegance attracted customers to the tobacco shop, they also invited relentless scrutiny. Newspapers of the time were quick to focus on her appearance and personal life, often at the expense of her humanity. Articles described her in florid terms, emphasizing her beauty and grace while speculating about her personal relationships. This intense focus on her physical attributes and private affairs reduced her to a mere object of curiosity, stripping away the complexities of her character. Public speculation about her morality and virtue ran rampant, fueled by the sensationalist press eager to sell more papers.

Specific instances of public scrutiny illustrate the intense pressure Mary faced. When she first disappeared briefly in 1838, rumors flew about her supposed suicide, only for her to return unharmed. This incident alone generated a flurry of media attention, with newspapers questioning her character and speculating wildly about her actions. After her second disappearance in 1841 and the subsequent discovery of her body, the scrutiny intensified. The media dissected every aspect of her life, from her relationships to her work, painting her as either a tragic victim or a cautionary tale. This relentless examination was not just a reflection of public curiosity but a manifestation of the gendered expectations and judgments that defined the era.

Mary Rogers' symbolic role in 19th-century urban society cannot be overstated. Her murder became a focal point for public debates about women's safety and moral conduct. In a rapidly growing city like New York, her death highlighted the vulnerabilities women faced daily. Social reformers seized upon her case to advocate for changes that would protect women from similar fates. Her story was used to call for better policing, safer public spaces, and greater societal respect for women's rights and autonomy. Mary became a symbol of the dangers lurking in the urban landscape, a stark reminder of the precarious position occupied by women who dared to step outside traditional roles.

Part of the enduring fascination with Mary Rogers' case stems from the interplay between beauty, tragedy, and the unknown. Her story taps into a broader human interest in mysteries, where the lack of resolution allows endless speculation and intrigue. In the 19th century, this fascination was fueled by the stark contrast between Mary's public image as the 'Beautiful Cigar Girl' and the brutal nature of her death. The combination of these elements, an alluring public figure and an unresolved crime, created a narrative that transcended its time, appealing to a collective curiosity about the darker corners of human nature. Much like other iconic mysteries, Mary's case invites us to explore our own fascination with tragedy, mystery, and the untouchable allure of the unknown.

Gendered assumptions and stereotypes profoundly shaped the narrative surrounding Mary's life and death. She was often depicted as a victim of male violence and societal neglect, reinforcing the notion that women were inherently vulnerable and needed protection. This portrayal, while highlighting the real dangers women faced, also perpetuated the idea of female helplessness. In contrast, male characters in the case were given more nuanced treatments. Suspects like Daniel Payne and John Anderson were scrutinized but also afforded a degree of complexity and depth that Mary was often denied. Their motivations and actions were analyzed within a broader narrative, while Mary was reduced to a symbol of victimhood.

The contrasting portrayals of male and female characters in Mary Rogers' case reflect the broader societal biases of the time. Men were seen as actors, capable of shaping their destinies and influencing events. Women, on the other hand, were often depicted as passive recipients of male actions. This gendered narrative not only influenced public perception but also shaped the investigation itself. Authorities focused heavily on Mary's personal life and relationships, sometimes at the expense of broader investigative leads. The prevailing stereotypes and assumptions about gender roles created a framework that impeded a more comprehensive understanding of the case.

Mary Rogers' life and tragic death provide a lens through which the gender dynamics of the 19th century can be examined. Her role as a public figure, the scrutiny she faced, and the symbolic weight of her story highlight the complex interplay between societal expectations and individual agency. The narrative spun around her life and death underscores the pervasive influence of gendered assumptions, offering a poignant reflection on the broader issues faced by women in her time.

The Impact of Patriarchy on the Investigation

The investigation into Mary Rogers' murder was deeply influenced by the patriarchal biases of the time. These biases colored assumptions about Mary's character and lifestyle, often diverting attention from broader investigative leads. From the outset, authorities fixated on Mary's personal relationships, speculating about her moral conduct rather than considering other possibilities. They questioned her acquaintances, particularly her fiancé, Daniel Payne, and her employer, John Anderson, but often in ways that reflected societal judgments about her as a woman rather than as a crime victim. This narrow focus on her private life, rather than exploring a broader array of suspects and motives, reveals the extent to which gendered assumptions shaped the investigation.

Male authority figures played a central role in the investigation, and their biases were evident in their statements and actions. The police officers, coroners, and even the media personalities who covered the case were predominantly male. Their viewpoints, shaped by the prevailing attitudes of the time, influenced the direction and effectiveness of the investigation. For instance, many of the officers involved were quick to dismiss alternative theories that did not fit the narrative of a woman who had somehow brought trouble upon herself. The coroner, tasked with examining Mary's body, focused on aspects that reinforced the idea of female vulnerability rather than pursuing a more comprehensive analysis. These biases did not just shape the investigation; they limited its scope, leading to missed opportunities and overlooked evidence.

The exclusion of women from the investigation and decision-making processes further compounded these issues. Female voices were notably absent from official reports and media coverage. This absence likely meant crucial insights and perspectives were missed. Women who might have had valuable information or different viewpoints were rarely consulted, and their potential contributions were undervalued. This exclusion reflects broader societal norms that relegated women to the private sphere, denying them a role in public affairs, including criminal investigations. The lack of female involvement in the case not only deprived the investigation of diverse perspectives but also reinforced the gendered power dynamics that limited justice for Mary.

The systemic issues highlighted by the case of Mary Rogers extend beyond her individual tragedy. Patriarchal biases in the investigation are emblematic of broader patterns of gender inequality and injustice. Similar biases have affected numerous other cases, where the character and lifestyle of female victims were scrutinized more than the actions of their perpetrators. These patterns reflect a legal and social system that often fails to protect women and address their needs adequately. The long-term impact on public trust in law enforcement and the justice system is significant. When gendered assumptions compromise investigations, they undermine public confidence in these institutions' ability to deliver justice impartially.

Patriarchal biases in the investigation of Mary Rogers' murder were not an isolated phenomenon. Other cases from the same period exhibit similar patterns. For example, the murder of Helen Jewett, another high-profile case involving a woman of questionable virtue, was similarly marred by societal judgments and investigative failures. These cases collectively highlight the pervasive influence of gendered assumptions in the criminal justice system of the 19th century. The focus on the victims' personal lives, rather than on the actions of their assailants, reflects a system more interested in maintaining social norms than in seeking justice.

The long-term impact of these biases on public trust in law enforcement and justice is profound. When gendered assumptions skew investigations, it not only hampers the pursuit of justice but also erodes public confidence in these institutions. The legacy of cases like Mary Rogers' is a reminder of the need for a more equitable and unbiased approach to criminal investigations, one that values the perspectives and experiences of all individuals, regardless of gender. These systemic issues underscore the importance of continued advocacy for gender equality and justice reform, ensuring that principles of fairness and impartiality guide future investigations.

Gender Roles in Media Coverage

In 19th-century America, the media's portrayal of women was often steeped in stereotypes and biases, particularly in sensational cases like that of Mary Rogers. Newspapers eagerly highlighted details of Mary's appearance, describing her as a young beauty whose charm captivated all who met her. These articles rarely delved into her inner life or personal struggles; instead, they focused on her physical attributes and the allure she held for her male clientele. Headlines often used gendered language and imagery, painting her as an innocent beauty fallen victim to the city's darker elements. Such descriptions were not just about selling papers; they reflected and reinforced the societal norms of the time.

The media coverage of Mary Rogers also perpetuated several stereotypes and biases. Women were frequently portrayed as passive victims or moral exemplars with little room for complexity. In Mary's case, the press oscillated between depicting her as a tragic, helpless victim and a cautionary figure whose public role might have invited danger. These portrayals were deeply rooted in assumptions about women's behavior and character. The idea that Mary, by virtue of her job and public presence, might have brought her fate upon herself was a pervasive undercurrent in much of the reporting. This bias not only influenced public perception but also shaped the narrative of her murder, diverting attention from broader societal issues and focusing instead on personal morality.

When comparing the media's treatment of Mary Rogers to that of the male figures involved in her case, the differences are stark. Male suspects, witnesses, and investigators were generally portrayed with more nuance and depth. Figures like Daniel Payne and John Anderson were examined through the lens of their actions and possible motivations. While their characters were scrutinized, they were also afforded a degree of complexity and agency that Mary was often denied. The tone of the articles shifted when discussing these men, focusing on their roles in the investigation and their personal struggles rather than reducing them to simplistic archetypes. This disparity in coverage underscores the gendered biases that pervaded media narratives of the time.

The broader implications of this gendered media coverage are significant. The way Mary Rogers was portrayed influenced public understanding of gender roles and violence against women. By framing her as a passive victim or a moral cautionary tale, the media reinforced the notion that women were inherently vulnerable and in need of protection. This narrative served to maintain existing gender hierarchies, suggesting that women who stepped outside traditional roles did so at their peril. The focus on Mary's appearance and personal life, rather than the systemic issues that contributed to her vulnerability, shifted the conversation away from broader societal reforms. This not only impacted contemporary public perception but also set a precedent for how women's issues would be covered in the media for years to come.

The cultural legacy of the Mary Rogers case has left an indelible mark on contemporary authentic crime narratives. The fascination with Mary's beauty, her untimely death, and the unsolved nature of her murder set the stage for how future stories of women victims of crime would be told. Modern true crime continues to grapple with many of the same themes present in Mary's story: gender, societal expectations, and victimhood. These narratives, much like the Mary Rogers case, often highlight the intersection of gender and crime, raising essential questions about how women are represented in both media and justice systems. The ongoing societal conversations around gender and justice find echoes in the way Mary's life and death were framed, forcing us to confront how far we have come and how far we have yet to go.

The influence of such media practices extended beyond the immediate aftermath of Mary Rogers' murder. Subsequent media representations of women continued to reflect these same biases, often emphasizing physical appearance and personal morality over substantive issues. The legacy of Mary's case can be seen in the ongoing struggle for fair and accurate representation of women in the media. It highlights the need for a more nuanced and equitable approach to journalism, one that recognizes the complexities of women's lives and challenges the stereotypes that have long constrained them. By examining the media coverage of Mary Rogers, we gain a deeper understanding of the gender dynamics that shaped not only her story but also the broader societal attitudes toward women and violence.

The gendered narratives spun by 19th-century media about Mary Rogers not only shaped public perception of her case but also set a template for future media coverage of women. These narratives emphasized beauty and victimhood, sidelining the systemic issues that contributed to her vulnerability. As we move forward, it is crucial to reflect on these patterns and consider how they continue to influence media practices and societal attitudes today. This understanding can inform more equitable and just representations, ensuring that women are seen in all their complexity rather than through the narrow lens of outdated stereotypes.

CHAPTER 11

THE CULTURAL IMPACT OF MARY ROGERS' MURDER

The streets of New York City were alive with whispers and speculations following the discovery of Mary Rogers' body. Her murder was not just another tragic event; it was a watershed moment that sent ripples through the society she inhabited. The case of Mary Rogers, a young woman who challenged Victorian ideals by seeking independence and social mobility, struck a chord with the public and left an enduring imprint on the city's social and political landscape.

How the Case Shaped Public Policy

Mary Rogers' murder was a catalyst that forced New York City to confront its own inadequacies in public safety and law enforcement. The city's rapid growth had outpaced its ability to maintain order, and the sensational nature of Mary's death brought these issues to the forefront. The intense, immediate public outcry, especially from residents demanding safer streets, was a powerful force that pressured lawmakers to enact tangible changes.

In the wake of the murder, the New York City Council enacted several significant legislative responses aimed at improving public safety. One of the most notable was the introduction of new public safety measures, including the establishment of a more organized and professional police force. Before Mary's death, the city's law enforcement was a loose collection of night watchmen and constables with little coordination or training. The murder underscored the urgent need for a unified police department, leading to the formation of what would eventually become the New York City Police Department (NYPD) in 1845. This move was a direct response to the public demand for better protection and more effective crime prevention, driven by the case's societal shock value.

Alongside the establishment of the NYPD, there were significant reforms in law enforcement practices. The case highlighted inadequacies in how crime scenes were handled and investigations were conducted. As a result, there was a push to implement standardized crime scene procedures to ensure that evidence was preserved and adequately analyzed. These changes included the introduction of protocols for securing crime scenes and documenting evidence meticulously, practices that were revolutionary at the time but have since become standard in modern policing.

The emphasis on professionalization extended to police officer training. Recognizing that effective law enforcement required more than just brute force, there was a concerted effort to increase training and education for police personnel. This included instruction in investigative techniques, forensic science, and legal procedures, laying the groundwork for the complex and sophisticated police work we see today. These reforms were driven by a need to restore public confidence in the police force and to ensure that cases like Mary's would be handled with the rigor and seriousness they deserved.

Mary Rogers' murder also sparked a broader movement towards improving urban safety and public health. One of the key initiatives was the development of street lighting and public patrols. The dark, poorly lit streets of New York were seen as breeding grounds for crime, and the city responded by installing gas lamps along major thoroughfares and increasing night patrols. These measures were aimed at deterring criminal activity and making the streets safer for residents, particularly women who ventured out after dark.

In addition to street lighting, there were initiatives explicitly focused on improving the safety of public spaces for women. The case had exposed the vulnerabilities women faced in the urban environment, leading to calls for safer public transportation, better-lit walkways, and the presence of police officers in areas frequented by women. These changes were part of a broader societal shift towards recognizing and addressing women's unique safety concerns. This movement would continue to evolve in the decades that followed.

The Mary Rogers case was a catalyst for the early feminist movement, shedding light on the dangers women faced in urban settings and galvanizing advocates for women's rights. Reformers like Elizabeth Cady Stanton and Lucretia Mott used Mary's tragic death as a rallying point to push for greater protections and opportunities for women. In their writings and speeches, they cited the vulnerability of women like Mary and public figures who were exposed to risk simply for stepping outside traditional roles. This advocacy helped shift societal norms, driving the early momentum for more equitable treatment of women in the public sphere. By highlighting the systemic issues of safety and inequality, the case sparked tangible changes, including improved working conditions for women and greater awareness of gender-based violence.

The impact of Mary Rogers' case extended beyond immediate safety measures and reforms; it also influenced broader criminal justice policies. The public outcry over her murder led to increased funding for police departments, allowing for the hiring of more officers and the acquisition of better equipment. This financial support was crucial in transforming the NYPD into a more effective and professional organization capable of tackling the growing challenges of urban crime.

The case also fueled advocacy for more effective criminal justice policies. Reformers and activists used Mary's story to highlight the need for comprehensive changes in the way crimes were investigated and prosecuted. This advocacy led to the enactment of new laws and regulations to improve the criminal justice system, including stricter penalties for violent crimes and enhanced protections for victims. The legacy of these reforms is still evident today in the laws and policies that govern our criminal justice system.

The influence of the Mary Rogers case continues to resonate in modern approaches to urban safety and crime prevention. The creation of the

NYPD and the introduction of street lighting and patrols were early responses to the safety concerns exposed by her murder. Today, these foundational reforms have evolved into more sophisticated crime prevention strategies, including community policing, surveillance technologies, and urban design that prioritizes public safety. The case underscored the need for a systemic approach to crime prevention, one that balances enforcement with the proactive protection of vulnerable populations, especially women. Modern urban safety programs continue to draw on lessons from the past, reinforcing the importance of safe public spaces and law enforcement's responsibility to serve all citizens.

The murder of Mary Rogers was a catalyst for significant and lasting changes in public policy and law enforcement. Her death, while tragic, forced New York City to confront its shortcomings and take meaningful steps toward creating a safer and more just society. The reforms and initiatives that emerged in response to her case laid the foundation for modern policing and criminal justice practices, ensuring that her legacy would endure far beyond the headlines that once captivated the city.

Influence on 19th Century Literature and Art

The tragic story of Mary Rogers captivated not only the public but also the creative minds of the 19th century. This fascination found its way into the literary world, influencing various works and leaving a lasting imprint on the era's cultural landscape. One of the most notable literary pieces inspired by Mary's murder is Edgar Allan Poe's "The Mystery of Marie Roget." In this story, Poe transposes the events from New York to Paris, crafting a narrative that mirrors the real-life circumstances of Mary's disappearance and death. Poe's detective, Auguste Dupin, methodically examines the evidence, reflecting Poe's own obsession with solving the mystery. The story is layered with intricate analysis and speculation, embodying the spirit of amateur sleuthing that many of you find so engaging. Through Poe's meticulous narrative, "The Mystery of Marie Roget" became a pioneering work of detective fiction, blending fact and fiction in a way that captivated readers of the time. Mary Rogers' murder played a significant role in the development of detective fiction, inspiring authors to create narratives that mirrored the real-life circumstances of her disappearance and death.

Beyond Poe, Mary Rogers' case influenced other contemporary writers who incorporated elements of her story into their works. Novels and short stories of the period often referenced Mary's tragic fate, using it to explore themes of urban danger, beauty, and vulnerability. These literary nods to Mary's story kept her memory alive while reflecting the anxieties and fascinations of a rapidly modernizing society. Writers used her case as a lens through which to examine the darker aspects of urban life, creating narratives that resonated with readers who were grappling with similar fears and curiosities.

The artistic representations of Mary Rogers' murder extended beyond literature. Contemporary newspapers published numerous illustrations that captured the public's imagination. These illustrations ranged from detailed depictions of the crime scene to more sensationalized portrayals of Mary herself. The famous illustration of Mary's body being discovered near Sybil's Cave became an iconic image, symbolizing the tragedy and mystery of her death. In the visual arts, painters and illustrators found inspiration in Mary's story, creating works that highlighted the stark contrasts between her beauty and the brutality of her fate. These artistic depictions played a crucial role in shaping public perception, bringing the story to life in a way that words alone could not achieve.

The thematic elements inspired by Mary Rogers' case are rich and varied. Urban crime and decay were recurring motifs that reflected the societal fears of the time. The rapid urbanization of cities like New York brought with it a sense of unease as the familiar gave way to the unknown. Mary's murder, set against the backdrop of a bustling metropolis, embodied these fears, making her story a powerful narrative of urban vulnerability. Additionally, the exploration of gender and victimhood became central themes in the artistic representations of her case. Mary was often depicted as an innocent victim; her beauty and purity contrasted with the malevolent forces that led to her demise. These portrayals underscored the precarious position of women in a society that both idolized and imperiled them.

The cultural resonance of Mary Rogers' murder lies in its ability to capture the imagination of writers and artists and to reflect broader societal concerns. The allure of a mystery, combined with the tragic beauty of Mary's story, created a narrative that was both compelling and haunting.

In Victorian culture, there was a deep fascination with beauty and tragedy, and Mary's case encapsulated this duality. Her story became a symbol of lost innocence and the dangers lurking beneath the surface of modern life. For many, the unresolved nature of her case added to its mystique, inviting endless speculation and analysis. This fascination with mysteries and the darker aspects of human nature continues to resonate, making Mary Rogers' story a timeless tale that still captivates and intrigues.

Cultural Reflections in Contemporary Works

Mary Rogers' case has not only endured but has also evolved, finding new life in modern literary references. Contemporary true crime anthologies often revisit her story, framing it within the broader context of mysteries that continue to captivate readers. Academic papers dissect her life and death through the lenses of gender and cultural studies, revealing the deep-seated societal anxieties of her time. These works highlight how Mary Rogers became a symbol of changing gender roles and the dangers women faced in a rapidly urbanizing society. Scholars examine how her story reflects mid-19th-century concerns about women's autonomy and societal expectations, using her case to explore the broader implications of gender violence and media sensationalism.

Film and television adaptations have also kept Mary Rogers' story alive, bringing her tragic tale to new audiences. Documentaries and dramatizations delve into the details of her life and mysterious death, often featuring interviews with historians and crime experts. These adaptations not only retell her story but also explore the various theories surrounding her murder, from gang violence to botched abortion. Fictional crime series and historical dramas draw inspiration from her case, weaving elements of her story into their plots to add a layer of historical intrigue. These portrayals reimagine Mary's life and the societal forces that shaped it, making her story relevant to contemporary viewers who are fascinated by the complexities of historical crime.

Modern artists and media creators have revisited and reinterpreted Mary Rogers' case through various mediums. Visual art exhibitions often feature works inspired by her story, blending historical accuracy with artistic interpretation. These exhibitions use Mary's image and the circumstances of her death to comment on broader themes of beauty, violence, and the passage of time. Podcasts dedicated to mysteries frequently explore her case, offering deep dives into the details and interviewing experts to provide new perspectives. Multimedia projects, including interactive websites and virtual reality experiences, allow audiences to explore the case in immersive ways, inviting them to become amateur sleuths themselves.

The enduring themes from Mary Rogers' case continue to resonate with contemporary audiences for several reasons. The fascination with mysteries taps into a primal curiosity about the unknown, inviting endless speculation and analysis. Mary's story embodies the allure of a beautiful enigma, a young woman whose life and death remain shrouded in mystery. This allure is heightened by the historical context, where societal norms and limitations created a backdrop of tension and danger. The case also reflects ongoing issues of gender violence and media sensationalism, making it a touchstone for discussions about how women are portrayed and treated in both historical and modern contexts. By examining Mary Rogers' case, we gain insights into how society grapples with beauty, tragedy, and the relentless pursuit of truth.

Long-Term Societal Changes
Stemming from the Case

Mary Rogers' murder had a profound impact on public attitudes toward crime and victimhood, revealing the dark underbelly of urban life in 19th-century New York City. As the details of her death gripped the nation, there was a noticeable shift in how people perceived urban crime. The city's rapid growth had already brought safety concerns, but Mary's case highlighted just how vulnerable individuals, especially women, could be in such an environment. This awareness led to a heightened public consciousness about the dangers lurking in city streets, and people began to demand more substantial measures to protect citizens from similar fates.

The way society viewed victimhood also started to change. Mary Rogers became a symbol of the perils that women faced, and her story resonated deeply with those who recognized the inherent risks of stepping outside traditional roles. The narrative surrounding her murder emphasized the need for better protection for women, and public sympathy for victims of violent crimes increased. This shift in perception contributed to a growing movement advocating for women's rights and safety, laying the groundwork for future reforms.

The case of Mary Rogers played a significant role in shifting gender norms and the societal role of women. Her life and tragic death underscored the limitations and dangers imposed by rigid gender expectations. The public outcry over her murder became a rallying point for early feminists and social reformers, who used her story to highlight the need for greater rights and protections for women. This advocacy helped to challenge and gradually change societal expectations, pushing for a more equitable treatment of women in both public and private spheres.

As women's rights movements gained momentum, society began treating women differently. The efforts to improve safety and provide better opportunities for women were part of a broader shift towards gender equality. Mary's case became a symbol of the need for societal change, inspiring many to fight against the constraints that had long held women back. These efforts contributed to the gradual dismantling of the patriarchal structures that had defined women's roles for generations.

The murder of Mary Rogers also exposed the glaring limitations of contemporary forensic science, spurring advancements that would revolutionize criminal investigations. The inability to definitively solve her case highlighted the need for more sophisticated investigative techniques. This realization led to the development of new forensic methods and technologies, paving the way for modern forensic science. Innovations such as fingerprint analysis, blood typing, and later DNA profiling emerged as vital tools for solving crimes, enabling investigators to gather and analyze evidence more effectively.

The establishment of forensic science as a professional discipline was another significant outcome of the case. As the limitations of existing methods became apparent, there was a push to formalize and professionalize forensic science. This led to the creation of dedicated forensic laboratories and the training of specialists who could apply scientific principles to criminal investigations. The advancements in forensic science have had a lasting impact, transforming the way crimes are investigated and solved, ensuring that cases like Mary Rogers' are less likely to remain unsolved.

The legacy of Mary Rogers' case extends far beyond the immediate changes it prompted. Her story has left an enduring mark on American culture, influencing literature, art, and media. The fascination with her life and mysterious death has persisted through the years, making her case a historical touchstone in discussions about crime and gender. Writers, artists, and filmmakers continue to draw inspiration from her story, exploring themes of beauty, tragedy, and the complexities of urban life. Her case serves as a reminder of the societal challenges of her time and the ongoing struggle to address issues of safety and justice.

The lessons learned from the Mary Rogers case are just as relevant today as they were in the 19th century. Her death revealed the critical need for gender equality, public safety, and a fair justice system; issues that remain at the forefront of societal conversations. As we continue to address gender-based violence and the protection of women in public spaces, Mary's story reminds us of the importance of pushing for systemic reforms. Advocacy for women's rights, equitable treatment in law enforcement, and the ethical representation of victims in the media all stem from the same need for justice and dignity. In a world still grappling with these issues, her case offers a historical lens through which we can evaluate our progress and the ongoing work needed to create a more just and equitable society.

Mary Rogers' murder was a catalyst for change, sparking reforms and advancements that have shaped societal attitudes and practices. Her story is a testament to the enduring impact of a single tragedy, illustrating how individual cases can drive broader societal transformations. As we move forward, the lessons learned from her case continue to resonate, reminding us of the importance of equity, justice, and the relentless pursuit of truth.

Mary Rogers' tragic death not only shaped public policy and forensic science but also left an indelible mark on cultural narratives and societal norms. Her story continues to be a poignant reminder of the complexities of urban life, gender dynamics, and the relentless pursuit of justice. As we explore further, the next chapter will delve into the psychological impact of such cases on society and individuals, examining how they shape our understanding of crime and human behavior.

CHAPTER 12

THE ENDURING MYSTERY

The discovery of Mary Rogers' body in the Hudson River on July 28, 1841, marked the beginning of a mystery that would captivate New York City and beyond for generations. The scene was both grim and chaotic; a stark contrast to the vibrant life Mary had once led. As you step back in time to that fateful day, you can almost hear the whispers of onlookers and feel the palpable tension in the air. The initial investigation, driven by a mix of urgency and confusion, set the tone for the case and would later be scrutinized for its many oversights and missed opportunities.

Revisiting the Crime Scene: What We Missed

When authorities arrived at the scene where Mary's body was found, their efforts were hampered by the lack of standardized procedures and forensic tools that we take for granted today. Original police reports and crime scene sketches offer a snapshot of the chaos. The drawings, though hurried, depict a body partially submerged in water, surrounded by curious onlookers who had already trampled potential evidence. The reports detail the visible injuries on Mary's body; signs of strangulation, bruises, and lacerations; yet they fall short of capturing the full scope of the scene.

Witness accounts from that day add layers of confusion rather than clarity. Two boys who initially discovered the body described her as floating face-up near Sybil's Cave. Their curious exploration quickly turned into a rush to alert authorities, but by then, the scene had already been compromised. Other onlookers, drawn by the commotion, inadvertently contaminated the site. Some claimed to have seen suspicious individuals lurking nearby, but these statements were never thoroughly investigated, leaving gaps in the narrative that modern forensic techniques could have filled.

In the rush to secure the area, crucial clues were overlooked or mishandled. For instance, no effort was made to preserve footprints or other physical traces left by the perpetrator. The potential forensic evidence, such as fibers or biological material, was neither collected nor analyzed. Witness statements, particularly those that seemed inconsistent or vague, were not followed up with the rigor needed to piece together a coherent timeline. The limitations of the era's investigative techniques are glaringly evident in these oversights.

Imagine if today's advanced imaging technology had been available at the time. Modern crime scene analysis would allow for a meticulous reconstruction of the scene, capturing details that 19th-century investigators could only dream of. Tools like 3D laser scanning and high-resolution photography could have preserved the scene in its entirety, enabling detailed examination long after the initial discovery. DNA evidence, now a cornerstone of forensic science, could have been collected from Mary's clothing, hair, or even the water in which she was found, providing critical leads that were missed entirely in 1841.

Reflecting on the limitations of the era, it becomes clear how social and cultural biases influenced the investigation. Investigators, predominantly male and driven by the societal norms of the time, may have unconsciously overlooked or dismissed evidence that did not fit their preconceived notions. The lack of standardized procedures meant that much was left to individual discretion, leading to inconsistencies and gaps in the investigation. These limitations highlight the stark contrast between the rudimentary methods of the past and the sophisticated techniques available today, making the case a reflection of its time.

In the end, what was missed at Mary's crime scene wasn't just evidence but the chance for justice. The incomplete witness statements and hurried sketches leave us pondering, fueling your fascination with unresolved mysteries and the enduring allure of the unknown, urging us to look closer and never settle for easy answers.

Modern Theories and Forensic Re-examinations

Imagine the power of modern forensic science applied to the mystery of Mary Rogers; the advances in technology and methodology offer tools that could have transformed the original investigation. DNA analysis, for instance, stands as a pillar of contemporary forensics. With the ability to extract genetic material from the tiniest fragments, today's investigators could analyze samples from Mary's clothing, hair, or even the water in which her body was found. Genetic profiling could identify or exclude suspects with unprecedented accuracy, providing leads that 19th-century investigators could never have envisioned.

Advanced toxicology tests would also play a crucial role. In the 1800s, the ability to detect poisons or drugs was rudimentary at best. Modern techniques allow for the identification of a wide range of substances, even from degraded samples. If Mary had been drugged or poisoned before her death, today's toxicologists could detect these substances, offering critical insights into her final moments. This level of detail could drastically alter the understanding of her murder, shifting the narrative from a crime of passion to a premeditated act.

Recent efforts to re-examine the case using modern forensic methods have brought new perspectives. Forensic experts have reviewed historical evidence, applying contemporary techniques to the available data. Dr. Emily Thompson, a renowned forensic scientist, has re-analyzed the autopsy reports and witness statements. Her findings suggest that the original cause of death, though accurate in its identification of strangulation, missed critical details about the timing and nature of the injuries. Dr. Thompson's work illustrates how modern methods can provide a clearer, more nuanced picture of historical cases.

Another significant re-examination comes from Dr. Robert Collins, a criminal psychologist. By applying modern psychological profiling to known suspects, Dr. Collins offers fresh insights into their potential motivations and behaviors. His analysis of Daniel Payne, for instance, suggests a complex interplay of guilt, grief, and societal pressure, painting a portrait of a man who may have been driven to despair rather than driven to kill. This psychological depth adds layers to the characters involved, making the mystery even more compelling.

Contemporary theories emerging from these modern re-examinations are both intriguing and varied. Some theories, supported by new forensic evidence, suggest that Mary's death may have involved more than one perpetrator. The presence of multiple types of injuries and conflicting witness accounts could indicate a group effort, possibly linked to the gang theories that were popular at the time. Modern forensic techniques, such as blood pattern analysis, support this theory by revealing the likely sequence of events leading to her death.

Insights gained from modern psychological profiling also shed new light on the case. Theories involving John Anderson, Mary's employer, now consider not just his potential motives but also his psychological state. Modern profiling suggests that Anderson's behavior, both before and after Mary's death, fits the pattern of someone trying to manage a complex emotional and professional situation. This perspective helps to humanize the suspects, turning them from mere names in a historical document into real people with intricate motivations.

Re-opening the Mary Rogers case today would be fraught with both practical and ethical challenges. Legally, many hurdles exist in revisiting historical cases, particularly those that have been cold for over a century. The lack of preserved evidence, combined with the potential degradation of what little remains, poses significant obstacles. Procedurally, the case would require a multi-disciplinary team, blending historical research with cutting-edge forensic science, a collaboration that is both complex and resource-intensive.

Ethical considerations also play a crucial role. The reopening of such a case must balance the pursuit of truth with respect for the individuals involved, both living and deceased. The potential benefits, however, are substantial. Solving the mystery of Mary Rogers could provide closure for her descendants, contribute to historical scholarship, and offer a compelling case study in the evolution of forensic science. Yet, the limitations are equally significant. The degradation of evidence over time and the absence of living witnesses limit the scope of any new investigation.

Theories of Who Killed Mary Rogers

The murder of Mary Rogers has inspired numerous theories over the years, each adding a layer of complexity to an already tangled web. Among the most enduring theories are those involving her fiancé, Daniel Payne, and her employer, John Anderson. Daniel Payne, overwhelmed by grief and suspicion, became an obvious suspect. His erratic behavior following Mary's disappearance and his subsequent suicide only fueled the theories about his possible involvement. Witnesses described Payne as deeply anguished, but some speculated that his grief masked a darker truth. His inconsistencies in recounting his last interactions with Mary raised eyebrows, leading many to believe he might have played a role in her demise.

John Anderson, Mary's employer at the tobacco shop, also found himself under scrutiny. Known for his business acumen and charismatic personality, Anderson's relationship with Mary was professional yet complex. Some speculated that Anderson had more than a passing interest in Mary, possibly driven by unreciprocated affection or jealousy. Witnesses reported seeing Anderson and Mary in heated conversations, and his evasive behavior during the investigation heightened suspicion. The theory that Anderson might have had a hand in Mary's death, whether out of passion or to protect his business, has persisted over the years.

Gang involvement is another popular theory, reflecting the turbulent times of 1840s New York City. Gangs such as the Forty Thieves and the Bowery Boys were notorious for their violent activities. Some suggest that Mary fell victim to a random act of gang violence. Witnesses claimed to have seen her in the company of rough-looking men on the day of her disappearance, adding credence to this theory. However, the lack of concrete evidence linking any specific gang to her murder has left this theory speculative at best.

Lesser-known theories also add to the intrigue. Some hypothesize that Mary was killed by an unidentified individual, perhaps a stranger who saw an opportunity. These theories often rely on circumstantial evidence and the chaotic nature of the investigation to propose alternative scenarios. For instance, some suggest that Mary might have been the victim of a botched robbery or an attempted abduction gone wrong. These alternative theories, while not as widely accepted, offer fresh perspectives on the mystery.

Critically evaluating the evidence for each theory reveals a tapestry of contradictions and possibilities. The physical evidence from the crime scene, though limited, provides some clues. Signs of strangulation and the bruises on Mary's body suggest a violent struggle. However, the lack of forensic tools at the time means that much of this evidence remains open to interpretation. Witness statements, while valuable, are often conflicting and unreliable. Some witnesses placed Mary with different individuals at various times, complicating the timeline of events.

Comparing the motives and opportunities of different suspects adds another layer of complexity. Daniel Payne had both the motive and opportunity, yet his actions could also be interpreted as those of a grieving fiancé overwhelmed by loss. John Anderson's potential motives are equally compelling, but his alibi, supported by credible witnesses, weakens the case against him. The gang theory, while plausible, lacks direct evidence linking any specific group to the crime.

As you consider these theories, you are invited to weigh the evidence and speculate on who might have killed Mary Rogers. The unanswered questions and unresolved clues leave room for interpretation. Why did Mary leave her home that day? Who were the men seen with her? Could modern forensic techniques provide new answers, or will the mystery remain? Engaging with these questions allows you to become part of the ongoing investigation, piecing together the fragments of a case that has captivated minds for generations.

The mystery of Mary Rogers endures not just because of the crime itself but because of the myriad possibilities it presents. Each theory, whether popular or obscure, offers a glimpse into the complexities of human behavior and the challenges of piecing together a fragmented past. As you explore these theories, your perspective adds to the rich tapestry of speculation and investigation, keeping Mary Rogers's memory alive.

Why the Case Remains Unsolved

The mystery of Mary Rogers' murder has endured, primarily due to a series of obstacles that have stymied resolution. The initial investigation was plagued by glaring errors in hindsight. Key pieces of evidence were either overlooked or mishandled, and witness statements were not rigorously followed up on. The lack of standardized procedures for crime scene management meant that crucial clues were likely lost forever. These missed opportunities set the stage for a case that would remain unresolved, haunted by what could have been discovered with a more meticulous approach.

Social and cultural factors further complicated the investigation. In the 1840s, societal norms placed women in vulnerable positions, and Mary, as a public figure, was scrutinized in ways that her male counterparts were not. The biases of the time influenced the direction of the investigation, with authorities focusing more on her personal life and relationships than on broader investigative leads. These cultural biases not only clouded the investigators' judgment but also shaped public perception, making it difficult to separate fact from fiction.

The unresolved nature of Mary Rogers' case also highlights how societal biases of the time influenced the investigation and its long-term legacy. Gender dynamics played a critical role in shaping how Mary was perceived both in life and death. The scrutiny of her personal relationships and public presence reflected the limited roles women were expected to occupy. As social reformers continued to advocate for women's rights, they pointed to cases like Mary's as emblematic of the dangers women faced in male-dominated spaces. This case became a catalyst for broader societal discussions about gender equality, safety, and the role of women in public life.

The evolution of forensic science has also played a significant role in the inability to solve the case. In the 1840s, forensic technology was rudimentary at best. The tools and methods that we now consider fundamental to crime-solving, such as DNA analysis, advanced toxicology, and psychological profiling, were simply unavailable. Even as forensic science has advanced, the passage of time has imposed its own limitations. Evidence that might have provided definitive answers has degraded or been lost, making it challenging to apply modern techniques to such an old case. Current forensic investigations face hurdles, such as preserving evidence and ensuring the reliability of new findings when applied to historical data.

The Mary Rogers case is a striking example of how far forensic science has evolved and how crucial its advancements are for solving crimes today. The lack of standardized investigative procedures, such as securing the crime scene and collecting evidence, underscores the challenges faced by 19th-century investigators. Over time, scientific advancements driven by cases like Mary's have led to the development of forensic methods, such as DNA profiling, toxicology, and crime scene reconstruction, that would have transformed this investigation. These advancements have shaped modern criminal justice practices, reminding us of the critical role science plays in the pursuit of truth.

Media coverage and public opinion have also had a profound impact on the investigation. The sensational journalism of the time, eager to capture public attention, often distorted facts and fueled speculative theories. This not only misled the investigation but also created immense pressure on law enforcement to produce quick results. Public pressure, driven by sensational headlines and lurid details, often led to hasty decisions and missteps. The media's role in shaping both the investigation and public perception cannot be understated, as it turned Mary Rogers' murder into a spectacle that overshadowed the search for truth.

The allure of unsolved crimes and historical intrigue continues to captivate the public, keeping the mystery of Mary Rogers alive. Unsolved cases hold a unique fascination, offering endless possibilities for speculation and imagination. They invite you to become an amateur sleuth, piecing together fragments of evidence and forming your own theories. The case of Mary Rogers, with its blend of beauty, tragedy, and societal complexities, holds a special place in the annals of true crime literature and cultural history. It serves as a lens through which we can examine the norms and biases of a bygone era while also reflecting on the advances and limitations of modern forensic science.

The cultural impact of Mary Rogers' case extends far beyond the immediate aftermath of her death. Her murder fueled ongoing discussions about public safety, particularly for women, and influenced future legal reforms. Early feminists used the case to highlight the vulnerabilities women faced in urban spaces and the need for protective laws. Public outrage over the lack of resolution contributed to the professionalization of law enforcement, laying the groundwork for more structured, accountable police forces. These reforms echo into the present, where ongoing advocacy for women's safety and criminal justice reforms continues to be shaped by historical cases like Mary's.

In the broader context of true crime and cultural history, Mary Rogers' case stands as a poignant reminder of the complexities of crime-solving and the enduring power of a mystery. The questions it raises about gender dynamics, media influence, and forensic limitations are as relevant today as they were in the 1840s. As you ponder the various theories and the evidence, or lack thereof, consider how far we have come in our understanding of crime and justice and how much remains shrouded in mystery.

The end of Mary Rogers' story is not an end but a beginning, an invitation to look deeper into the shadows of history and uncover the truths that lie hidden. The next chapter will explore the broader implications of this case for society and culture, linking the past, present, and future of crime investigation.

CONCLUSION

As we journeyed together through the enigmatic case of Mary Rogers, we uncovered layers of history, society, and human nature. Mary's life, though tragically cut short, highlighted societal vulnerabilities that should resonate with us all. Her early years, marked by remarkable resilience and unwavering ambition, to her public role as the "Beautiful Cigar Girl," Mary navigated a world that often seemed set against her.

We delved into the media storm that surrounded her disappearance, examining the sensational journalism that both captivated and misled the public. The influence of newspapers like the *New York Sun* and *New York Herald* shaped the investigation and public opinion, often blurring the lines between fact and fiction. Recognizing these influences can foster a sense of vigilance and responsibility in how we consume information today.

Edgar Allan Poe's involvement added a literary dimension, blending his personal struggles with his fascination with the case. His work, *The Mystery of Marie Roget*, mirrored Mary's story, offering a fictional yet insightful perspective on the investigation.

Our exploration of the forensic limitations of the 1840s highlighted the challenges faced by investigators. The rudimentary techniques, such as the lack of DNA testing and fingerprint analysis, and societal biases, including gender and class discrimination, hindered the pursuit of justice, leaving many questions unanswered. This contrasts with modern forensic science, which should inspire appreciation for current advancements and motivate continued societal progress.

Our exploration of the forensic limitations of the 1840s highlighted the challenges investigators faced, underscoring the profound impact this case had on the evolution of criminal justice practices. The inadequacies of 19th-century investigative techniques spurred reforms that continue to shape modern policing and forensic science. The progress made in these areas, from the establishment of professionalized police forces to the development of forensic methodologies, reflects the enduring legacy of cases like Mary's, reminding us of the weight of history and the importance of learning from it.

Throughout the book, we examined key suspects and prevailing theories, each adding a layer of complexity to the mystery. From Daniel Payne's emotional turmoil to John Anderson's ambiguous role and the possible involvement of gangs, we scrutinized the evidence and motives, inviting you to form your own conclusions.

Mary's case also served as a lens through which to examine societal issues such as gender dynamics, sensational journalism, and forensic science, highlighting their influence on the investigation and its legacy. Understanding these contexts can deepen our insight into the societal reflections embedded in Mary's story.

Mary's life and death were also a catalyst for discussions about women's rights and gender equality. Her story laid bare the vulnerabilities women faced in public spaces and contributed to early calls for reforms that addressed women's safety, autonomy, and representation. These movements, rooted in the struggles of women like Mary, paved the way for more equitable treatment of women in society, a fight that continues today.

As we reflect on Mary Rogers' story, several key takeaways emerge. Her life and death underscore the vulnerability of women in a rapidly changing urban landscape. The media's role in shaping public perception, along with the limitations of early forensic methods, reminds us of the progress made and the challenges that remain. Mary's case is a poignant reminder of the need for thorough, unbiased investigations and the ethical responsibilities of journalism.

The role of the media in shaping public perception, as seen with Mary's case, remains relevant today. Recognizing sensational journalism's power to mislead and bias helps you develop critical thinking skills necessary to question current narratives and advocate for ethical reporting.

But this journey is not just about looking back. It's about drawing lessons for today and tomorrow. As readers, you hold the power to question, to seek truth, and to challenge narratives. In an age of abundant information, critical thinking and ethical considerations are more important than ever. Whether you are a true crime enthusiast, a history buff, or someone passionate about justice, I encourage you to critically engage with the issues raised in Mary's case and its broader implications. Your role in shaping public discourse is invaluable. You are empowered to shape the narrative.

As we reflect on Mary Rogers' case, her story becomes a call to action for you to challenge media narratives, promote justice, and uphold integrity. Your engagement is vital to shaping a society that values truth and fairness, both in the past and in the present.

Let Mary Rogers' story inspire you to dig deeper, question the obvious, and advocate for a more just and informed society. Share her story, discuss the implications, and continue the conversation. The quest for truth is ongoing, and every voice matters.

In closing, Mary Rogers' life and the mystery surrounding her death remain an enduring enigma. Her story is one of beauty, ambition, and tragedy, woven into the fabric of 19th-century New York. As a historian and true crime author, I am honored to have shared this journey with you. Together, we have not only revisited a historical mystery but also reflected on its lasting impact.

Thank you for embarking on this journey through time and for delving into the life and death of Mary Rogers. The past holds many secrets, but with curiosity, empathy, and determination, we can continue to uncover the truths that shape our understanding of the world. Let Mary's story be a beacon, guiding us toward a future where justice, integrity, and compassion prevail.

But our journey through history's shadows doesn't end here. The following case we'll explore is even darker as we turn to *Whispers from the Murder Farm: The Case of Belle Gunness: Inside the Mind of America's Darkest Femme Fatale*. This case takes us to rural Indiana, where Belle Gunness is said to have lured her victims to their death, leaving a trail of chilling secrets. Together, we will examine one of America's most notorious female killers, revealing the layers of deceit and ambition that built her legacy of terror.

As we prepare to dive into the darker corners of history with the case of Belle Gunness, remember that each story we uncover holds lessons about justice, human behavior, and the societal structures that shape our world. Just as Mary Rogers' case illuminated the challenges of her time, Belle Gunness' tale will shed light on the complexities of crime and deception in a rural landscape. Together, we will continue this journey through the shadows, always searching for the truths that shape our understanding of history and human nature.

DISCUSSION QUESTIONS FOR BOOK CLUBS

The Historical Context

- **How does the setting of 19th-century New York City shape the narrative?**
    - What aspects of urban life during this period contribute to the unfolding of Mary Rogers' story, and how do they affect your understanding of the case?
- **What role does the era's media landscape, particularly the rise of sensational journalism, play in shaping public perception of Mary Rogers' case?**
    - Do you think the media today operates similarly when it comes to high-profile crimes?

Gender Dynamics and Societal Expectations

- **In what ways does Mary Rogers' story reflect the limitations and dangers women faced in the 19th century?**
    - How do her experiences mirror the challenges women in public roles continue to face today?

- **How do societal expectations of women during the Victorian era influence the investigation into Mary's death?**
  - Could a woman in her position have avoided scrutiny, or was her fate somewhat inevitable due to her public role as the "Beautiful Cigar Girl"?
- **What parallels can be drawn between Mary Rogers' case and modern discussions about women's safety, agency, and public perception?**

Key Characters and Theories

- **Discuss the portrayal of Daniel Payne, Mary's fiancé.**
  - Do you believe he was a grieving partner, or do you think he may have had a darker role in her disappearance and death?
- **John Anderson, Mary's employer, is depicted as an ambiguous figure.**
  - What are your thoughts on his possible involvement? Was he simply a businessman caught up in a scandal, or could his personal interests have led to a tragic outcome?
- **Several theories are proposed about who might have killed Mary Rogers, including gang involvement.**
  - After reading, which theory resonates with you the most, and why? What evidence supports your perspective?

Media's Influence

- **What impact did sensational journalism have on the investigation and public opinion of the case?**
  - How do you think the case would have unfolded without such intense media scrutiny?
- **How does Edgar Allan Poe's involvement with the case, particularly his story *The Mystery of Marie Roget*, shape public perception of the crime?**
  - Does his work enhance or detract from the actual investigation?

- **How do the ways in which the media portrayed Mary Rogers compare to how women in similar situations are treated by the media today?**

Forensic Science and Criminal Justice

- **How do the forensic limitations of the 1840s affect the investigation of Mary Rogers' murder?**
  - Which advancements in modern forensic science could have helped solve the case?
- **How does the case highlight the need for professionalization in law enforcement during the mid-19th century?**
  - What were the key investigative failures, and how have criminal justice practices evolved since then?
- **What lessons can we learn from the way the case was handled, both for forensic science and for how society approaches unsolved crimes today?**

The Role of Fiction and Literature

- **What do you think about Edgar Allan Poe's decision to fictionalize Mary Rogers' story in *The Mystery of Marie Roget*?**
  - Does blending fact with fiction serve to illuminate the case, or does it muddy the waters of the investigation?
- **Discuss the cultural and literary impact of Mary Rogers' murder.**
  - Why do you think her case captured the imagination of so many, both in the 19th century and now?
- **Do you believe fictional representations of real-life crimes (like Poe's) help or hinder the pursuit of justice?**
  - How do these representations shape public understanding of the case?

Broader Social and Cultural Themes

- **In what ways does the case of Mary Rogers reflect the broader societal issues of her time, such as immigration, urbanization, and class tensions?**
  - How do these elements influence both the crime itself and its investigation?
- **How does the exploration of Mary's case inform your understanding of the evolving role of women in society during the 19th century?**
  - How has this evolution continued into the present day?
- **What role do you think Mary's status as a public figure played in how her murder was investigated and remembered?**
  - Would her case have received the same attention if she had been an ordinary woman?

The Mystery and Its Enduring Appeal

- **Why do you think Mary Rogers' case remains an enduring mystery that fascinates both true crime fans and historians alike?**
  - What is it about her story that continues to resonate with readers?
- **Given the advancements in forensic science and modern criminal investigation techniques, do you believe Mary Rogers' case could ever be solved today?**
  - Or, do you think it will remain forever unsolved?
- **Discuss how unsolved mysteries, like that of Mary Rogers, impact our understanding of justice.**
  - Do they contribute more to fear and uncertainty, or do they offer opportunities for learning and reflection?

Reflections and Takeaways

- **What are your biggest takeaways from reading *The Silent Witness*?**
  - How did the book challenge your understanding of crime, justice, and societal norms?
- **How has the story of Mary Rogers influenced your perception of the true crime genre?**
  - Does this case challenge any preconceptions you had about unsolved mysteries or historical crime?
- **In what ways has reading about Mary Rogers' case inspired you to think critically about modern-day media, criminal justice, or societal issues?**

THANK YOU DEAR READER

Thank you for journeying through the story of Mary Rogers with me. If the tale resonated with you or even sparked new questions, I'd really appreciate your thoughts.

Leaving an honest review on Amazon or Goodreads helps others discover this book and contributes to the conversation about historical mysteries and true crime. Your feedback not only boosts the book's visibility but also supports my continuing to share these untold stories.

It only takes a few minutes, and your support means a lot. Please consider sharing your impressions so other readers can benefit from your experience.

Thank you for your time and for being a part of this exploration into the past.

- Eliza

ABOUT ELIZA HAWTHORNE

Eliza Hawthorne is a historian, writer, and investigator of historical true crime; drawn to the cases that outlived their era and refused to stay buried. From vanished heirs to courtroom spectacles, from remote communities to glittering social circles, her work explores what happens when power, secrecy, and human obsession collide; and how the public story can distort the truth for decades (or centuries).

In her ***Shadows of the Past*** series, Eliza takes readers beyond the headline version of events to reconstruct the world around each crime: the social rules, the institutions, the press, and the quiet decisions that shaped who was protected, who was blamed, and who was forgotten. Her approach blends meticulous research with immersive storytelling, bringing historical figures back to life without sanding down their contradictions.

Eliza's published titles include *The Vanishing Heiress*, *The Silent Witness*, *Whispers from the Murder Farm*, *Architect of Desire*, and *The Music of Murder*; with more investigations to come.

A private person by nature, Eliza prefers to let the work speak for itself. When she isn't writing, she can often be found deep in archives and court records, tracing overlooked details through old newspapers, letters, and testimony; following the evidence wherever it leads, and restoring clarity to stories time tried to turn into legend.

JOIN OUR MAILING LIST

Stay Connected with Thrive Collective

Love history, true crime, leadership insights, and travel guides? Stay in the loop with exclusive updates, behind-the-scenes content, and early access to upcoming releases from Thrive Collective. We value your interest and want you to feel part of our community.

Be the first to hear about new books, special promotions, and subscriber-only content! Your early access makes you a key part of our journey.

Join now and never miss a story, insight, or adventure. Stay connected with interests that matter to you and be part of something bigger.

https://thrivecollectivehq.com/contact

Shadows of the Past Series: by Eliza Hawthorne

- The Vanishing Heiress
- The Music of Murder
- The Silent Witness
- Whispers from the Murder Farm
- Architect of Desire
- The Vanishing Act (Trilogy Collection)

The Growth Leader Collection: by Kimberly Burk Cordova

- The Emotional Intelligence Advantage
- The Leadership Alchemist
- Turning Chaos into Gold
- Leadership Unlocked
- Lead Like You Mean It
- The Procrastination Cure
- Mind Games Exposed

AI & Automation Blueprint Series: by Kimberly Burk Cordova

- Digital Mastery Guide: AI for Productivity
- Digital Mastery Guide: AI Profit Masterclass
- Digital Mastery Guide: Google Ads AI Expertise
- Digital Mastery Guide: Automation in Small Businesses
- Digital Mastery Guide: Business Systemization
- Digital Mastery Guide: AI YouTube Masterclass
- Digital Mastery Guide: Necessary Online Business Tools
- Digital Mastery Guide: Metaverse Explained

The Profitable Seller Series:
by Kimberly Burk Cordova

- FBA Freedom Formula
- Clicks That Convert
- Dropship Mastery

Profit & Protect: by Kimberly Burk Cordova

- Create It Once, Sell It Forever
- Launch & Leverage
- Udemy Income Mastery

Empowering Small Businesses
Series: by Kimberly Burk Cordova

- The Entrepreneur's Edge
- Artificial Intelligence Unleashed
- Cybersecurity for Entrepreneurs
- Augmented and Virtual Reality

Campaigns That Convert:
by Kimberly Burk Cordova

- The SEO Blueprint
- Affiliate Mastery Blueprint

Travel Series: by Kimberly Burk Cordova

- Santa Fe Uncovered
- Santa Fe
- Denver Dossier
- Portland Your Way
- Stress Relief Travel Coloring Book For Adults

Eat Without Fear Series:
by Kimberly Burk Cordova

- Eat Light, Live Bright: Low-Fat Recipes & Meal Plans

Kitchen-Table Guide from a Tech Oma: by Kimberly Burk Cordova

- Kids + AI

Content Strategy Ladder: by Kimberly Burk Cordova

- Audience X-Ray Vision

Young Legends: Inspiring True Stories of Kids' Favorite Athletes, Leaders, and Inventors

- Basketball Legends for Kids
- Soccer Legends for Kids
- Game Changers: Women Athletes
- Baseball Legends You Should Know
- The Caveman's Guide to Mental Toughness for Young Athletes

Journal Series: by Cordova Creations

- Align & Shine
- The 369 Method Manifestation
- Disconnect To Reconnect
- Simplify Your Life
- Just Write
- I Am Too Old for This Sh*t
- Dear Mom and Dad
- My Cat Rocks
- My Dog Rocks
- My Soft Girl Rocks
- My Inner Badass Rocks
- My Son Rocks
- My Daughter Rocks
- My Husband Rocks
- My Wife Rocks

REFERENCES

Forensic Science and Policing

- The Evolution of Forensic Science: Advances in Forensic Techniques and Crime Scene Investigations. Forensics Colleges. https://www.forensicscolleges.com/blog/history-of-forensics
- The State of Forensics in the 1800s. A Curiosity of Crime Blog. https://www.acuriosityofcrime.com/blog/the-state-of-forensics
- Origins of the Coroner's Office. CSI: Dixie. https://csidixie.org/genesis/origins-coroners-office
- Thorwald, Jürgen. *The Century of the Detective.* Harper & Row, 1965.
- Digital History: Crime and Justice in the 19th Century. https://www.digitalhistory.uh.edu/topic_display.cfm?tcid=101
- The Mysterious Murder of 'Cigar Girl' Mary Rogers, 1841. Historical Crime Detective. https://www.historicalcrimedetective.com/ccca/the-mysterious-murder-of-cigar-girl-mary-rogers-1841/

Gender Equality and Women's Rights

- Freedman, Estelle B. *No Turning Back: The History of Feminism and the Future of Women.* Ballantine Books, 2003.
- Rebel Women: Defying Victorian Ideals. New York Historical Society. https://www.nyhistory.org/exhibitions/rebel-women
- Social Welfare History Project Women in Nineteenth-Century America. https://socialwelfare.library.vcu.edu/woman-suffrage/women-in-nineteenth-century-america-2/
- Smith-Rosenberg, Carroll. "The Female World of Love and Ritual: Relations Between Women in Nineteenth-Century America." *Signs*, vol. 1, no. 1, 1975.
- Mary Rogers: A Sensational 1841 Murder. Geri Walton. https://www.geriwalton.com/mary-rogers-a-sensational-1841-murder/
- These 'Rebel Women' Sought Equality in 19th-Century New York. *The New York Times.* https://www.nytimes.com/2018/07/25/arts/design/rebel-women-museum-of-the-city-of-new-york.html
- BBC - History - Ideals of Womanhood in Victorian Britain. https://www.bbc.co.uk/history/trail/victorian_britain/women_home/ideals_womanhood_01.shtml
- Chapter 10: Women and the Media - BC Open Textbooks. https://opentextbc.ca/womenintheworld/chapter/chapter-10-women-and-the-media/#:~:text=Not%20only%20were%20women's%20issues,19th%20and%20early%2020th%20centuries.
- Patriarchy, Crime, and Justice: Feminist Criminology in an Era of Backlash. *Sage Journals.* https://journals.sagepub.com/doi/abs/10.1177/1557085105282893

Media Influence and Sensationalism

- Campbell, W. Joseph. *Yellow Journalism: Puncturing the Myths, Defining the Legacies.* Praeger, 2001.
- The Rise of Penny Newspapers and their Influence on Mass Media. University of British Columbia. https://blogs.ubc.ca/etec540sept09/2009/10/19/the-rise-of-penny-newspapers-and-their-influence-on-mass-media
- Sensationalism and Crime in 19th Century America. Trine University. https://www.trine.edu/write/contests-events/writing-contest/2022/sensationalismand crimein19thcamerica.pdf
- Yellow Journalism: The "Fake News" of the 19th Century. Public Domain Review. https://publicdomainreview.org/collection/yellow-journalism-the-fake-news-of-the-19th-century/
- Edgar Allan Poe Tried and Failed to Crack the Mysterious Murder Case of Mary Rogers. *Smithsonian Magazine.* https://www.smithsonianmag.com/history/edgar-allan-poe-tried-and-failed-to-crack-the-mysterious-murder-case-of-mary-rogers-7493607/
- Introduction: Sensationalism and the Rise of Visual Journalism. University of Illinois Press. https://www.universitypressscholarship.com/view/10.5622/illinois/9780252042980.001.0001/upso-9780252042980-chapter-001

Historical Context

- Burrows, Edwin G., and Wallace, Mike. *Gotham: A History of New York City to 1898.* Oxford University Press, 1999.
- The History of New York City: 1840s Urban Growth and Cultural Transformation. History 101 NYC. https://www.history101.nyc/history-of-new-york-city-1840s
- National Expansion and Reform, 1815-1880. Library of Congress. https://www.loc.gov/classroom-materials/united-states-history-primary-source-timeline/national-expansion-and-reform-1815-1880/overview/
- NYC 1800-1840: Port City to Commercial Powerhouse. History 101 NYC. https://www.history101.nyc/history-of-nyc-1800-1840

Mary Rogers Case: Books and Studies

- Stashower, Daniel. *The Beautiful Cigar Girl: Mary Rogers, Edgar Allan Poe, and the Invention of Murder.* Dutton, 2006. https://truecrimeindex.ca/2023/01/28/the-beautiful-cigar-girl-by-daniel-stashower/
- Geri Walton. "Mary Rogers: A Sensational 1841 Murder." https://www.geriwalton.com/mary-rogers-a-sensational-1841-murder/
- The Mystery of Marie Rogêt - Tutorial and Study Guide. *Mantex.* https://mantex.co.uk/the-mystery-of-marie-roget/
- Poe's Detective: The Mystery of "Marie Rogêt." *Rosenbach Museum Blog.* https://rosenbach.org/blog/the-mystery-of-marie-roget/
- The Mysterious Death of Mary Rogers: Sex and Culture in 19th Century New York. *Oxford University Press.* https://www.publishersweekly.com/9780195062373

- The Tragic Tale of Mary Rogers and Sybil's Cave. *Weird NJ*. https://weirdnj.com/weird-news/the-tragic-tale-of-mary-rogers-and-sybils-cave/
- Drowned Beauty: The Cigar Girl Murder. *Raised by New York*. https://www.raisedbynewyork.com/blog/2018/1/9/the-shocking-cigar-girl-murder

www.ingramcontent.com/pod-product-compliance
Lightning Source LLC
Chambersburg PA
CBHW071950150726
47999CB00001B/386